INTRODUCTION

The fourteenth century in England was a period of religious conflict and war with France; it saw severe economic depression, notably between the years 1315 and 1317, and the first and most devastating appearance of the Black Death, in 1348-49. The relevance of these events to the 'peasants' uprising, which occurred mainly in the south-eastern counties in May-July 1381, is a matter of debate.

Economic depression and particularly the bubonic plague had the effect of reducing the labour force and driving up wages. The government sought to control wages at the 1346 level, first by a royal ordinance of 1349, and then in 1351 by the Statute of Labourers, which also placed other restrictions on the freedom of workers. Although this policy was not generally effective, the rising of 1381 seems to have occurred with most violence in those counties where the Statute was most strictly enforced. It may be significant too that one of the effects of the Hundred Years War with France was a very real threat of French invasion, which contributed to the general restlessness of the south-eastern counties.

The cost of the war, moreover, caused the government to introduce in 1377 a new form of taxation, the poll-tax. This was a levy of one groat for each person of either sex over the age of fourteen years: paupers and mendicant friars were exempted; beneficed clergy were to pay three groats. Second and third poll-taxes which followed in 1379 and 1381 were graded according to social class. There is ample evidence that these taxes were strongly resented and widely evaded, and that their imposition was a major factor leading to the rebellion. "Open defiance of the tax commissioners apparently first led to outright rebellion in three marshland villages near Brentwood, from which it soon spread to the rest of the county of Essex. The men of Essex rapidly developed considerable cohesion and esprit de corps; but contemporaries were much more alarmed by the greater initiative, determination and coordination soon displayed by the rebels of Kent. Although it is impossible to know exactly when and where it was taken, the decision to march on London was crucial and brought a startled government into a state of near panic. Under the guidance of Wat Tyler, John Ball and other leaders, the Kentishmen were never again quite so united or successful as during their long walk from Canterbury to Blackheath on 11 and 12 June".*

The crucial events of the rising took place in London during the next three days. The rebels from Kent and Essex, entered the city on Thursday, 13 June, and sacked and burned the Savoy — the residence of the Duke of Lancaster — Temple Bar, the Hospital of St. John at Clerkenwell, and many other properties. On the next day, Friday, the young king Richard II confronted the rebels at Mile End, where he received their expressions of loyalty, listened to their grievances, and gave certain undertakings to reform their status and conditions. While this meeting was in progress a group of the rebels made their way to the Tower of London, seized several eminent persons including Simon of Sudbury, archbishop of Canterbury, and Sir Robert Hales, Treasurer of England and High Prior of the Hospital of St. John at Clerkenwell, and beheaded them on Tower Hill.

It was during the night of 13-14 June that the news of the rising first reached St. Albans

*R. B. Dobson, ed. *The Peasants' Revolt of 1381.* Macmillan, 1970.

(see p. 86), and the people of St. Albans began their own march to London in the early hours of Friday morning. While in London their leaders had meetings both with the king and with Wat Tyler, the leader of the rebels. Réville speculates that their encounter with Richard probably occurred at Mile End, no doubt on the Friday afternoon. It seems that the meeting with Wat Tyler must also have occurred during that afternoon, since William Grindecob and William Cadingdone, leaders of the St. Albans rebels, were apparently back in St. Albans by nightfall.

On the afternoon of Saturday, 15 June, the king summoned the rebels to a further meeting at Smithfield. There, at the king's invitation, Wat Tyler recounted the rebels' demands, and received assurances that as many as possible would be granted. Then, before he could return to the ranks of his supporters, Tyler became involved in a scuffle with some of the king's retinue, in the course of which he received a mortal wound. It seems that young Richard II himself then prevented a riot by riding towards the body of the rebels, calling upon them to reassemble in Clerkenwell Fields nearby, whence they were peacefully dispersed. The news of Tyler's death reached St. Albans at daybreak on the following morning (see p. 95).

This brief introduction has provided no more than a framework and background for the papers which follow. It has not attempted to summarize in any comprehensive way the national history of the revolt of 1381. The extract from André Réville's account, which has not previously been translated into English, discusses the course of the revolt in Hertfordshire, the aims and motives of the Hertfordshire rebels, and — with Hertfordshire as an example — the actions taken by the government after Wat Tyler's death.

THE RISING OF THE WORKERS OF HERTFORDSHIRE IN 1381

by
André Réville

André Réville's *Le Soulèvement des Travailleurs d'Angleterre en 1381* was first published in Paris in 1898, four years after the author's death. The volume was edited by Professor Petit-Dutaillis, who provided some additional footnotes, identified here by the use of square brackets.

Professor R. B. Dobson has written as follows:

"A satisfactorily large scale and detailed history of the revolt is still lacking. The author who came nearest to achieving this aim was the young André Réville, from whose death at the age of twenty-seven the study of the Peasants' Revolt seems at times never to have recovered".*

Réville was not free of the class prejudices of his time, and some of his assessments may now need to be reconsidered. Nevertheless his thoroughly researched work, based on a comprehensive study of contemporary sources, and told in a powerful narrative style, remains one of the most satisfying accounts of the rising, particularly in regard to the events in Hertfordshire.

The present translation by Arthur Jones of the Hertfordshire sections of this work is published by kind permission of the Société de l'École des Chartes, Paris.

*Dobson. *Op. cit.*

Foreword

In Hertfordshire the revolt was less spontaneous than in Essex and Kent. There, the peasants had risen up of their own accord, and after a quiet beginning everyone was up within a fortnight and marching on London. The people of Hertfordshire, Cambridge-shire, Norfolk and Suffolk were merely following this lead. They admired the boldness of their brothers, and, since they suffered from the same ills, tried to copy them. Walsing-ham, or the author — whoever he was for this period — of *Chronicon Angliae* and of the *Historia Anglicana*, reported that the inhabitants of the various counties received news immediately of the revolt in Essex and Kent;[1] and the chronicler at Dunstable said more specifically that when the people of St. Albans and Barnet learned that their fellows in Kent, Essex and London had risen against the king and imposed their will upon him, they rose up similarly against their lord, the Abbot of St. Albans.[2]

Since Hertfordshire lies to the north of London, the insurrection spread naturally from south to north. On 13 June, the day of the Feast of the Consecration, just when the companions of Jack Straw, John Ball and Wat Tyler penetrated into London by way of Aldgate and London Bridge, their shouting and cheering were echoed in the extreme south of Hertfordshire, in the town of Barnet, and from there in the evening the revolt spread to St. Albans. On that fertile soil of rebellions the seed of revolt, once sown, might be expected to germinate easily.

References, Foreword

1. *Chronicon Angliae, auctore monacho quodam S. Albani*, p. 286. Also in *Thomae Walsingham Historia Anglicana*, I, 455.
2. *Annales de Dunstaplia*, p. 416-417.

List of Abbreviations used

Annales de Dunstaplia	*Annales prioratus de Dunstaplia.* Rolls Series. HMSO, 1858.
Chron. Angl.	*Chronicon Angliae, ab anno domini 1328 usque ad annum 1388: auctore monacho quodam Sancti Albani,* edited by E. M. Thompson. Rolls Series. HMSO, 1874.
Gesta	Walsingham, Thomas. *Gesta abbatum monasterii Sancti Albani,* edited by H. T. Riley. Rolls Series. HMSO, 3 vols., 1867-9.
Hist. Anglic.	Walsingham, Thomas. *Historia Anglicana,* edited by H. T. Riley. Rolls Series. HMSO, 2 vols., 1863-4.
Knighton	*Chronicon Henrici Knighton,* edited by J. R. Lumby. Rolls Series. HMSO, 2 vols., 1889-95.
Rymer	Rymer, Thomas. *The new Foedera.* Record Commision. 3 vols., 1816-30.
Polychronicon	*Polychronicon Ranulphi Higden,* edited by C. Babbington. Rolls Series. HMSO, 9 vols., 1865-86.
Vita Ricardi	*Historia vitae regni Ricardi,* edited by Thomas Hearne. Oxford 1729.

CHAPTER 1. THE RISING OF THE TOWNSPEOPLE OF ST. ALBANS

St. Albans abbey, of royal foundation,[1] was one of the most powerful monastic houses —
perhaps *the* most powerful — in all England. It exercised an extremely wide dominion, first
over the whole of the liberty of St. Albans or the Hundred of Cashio, then over a multitude
of manors scattered throughout Hertfordshire as well as in the neighbouring counties of
Buckinghamshire, Bedfordshire, Middlesex and Essex. The head of this monastery was a
very important personage indeed.

But this undoubted power encountered some resistance. The abbot, who was a sovereign on a small scale, lacked the common touch, and relations with his subjects were
strained. He exercised his seignorial rights with extreme vigour, would not allow his free
tenants to buy villein land or his serfs to buy freehold property, demanded without any
remission the rents and services which were owed to him, sought out and punished those
who tried to escape payment, and punished with the utmost severity anyone who hunted in
the immense warrens reserved for the use of the monastery.[2] The population of St. Albans
were living in a state of chronic tension, and there were continual riots against the religious
community.

In 1274 the townspeople, contesting the rights of the abbot, resolved to accept no longer
the obligation attaching to their servile status to grind their corn at the monastery's mill but
to set up hand querns in their houses for that purpose. Abbot Roger de Norton seized their
querns. Then the rebels levied a general contribution from all, poor and rich alike, to
establish a resistance fund. Serious troubles blew up. But force of arms, the supreme
argument in a time of anarchy, had the last word, and the abbey was confirmed in all its
rights.

In 1314 there were again disturbances in the town, and for many years the sovereignty of
the monastery was an illusion. In 1326 the people of St. Albans built a scaffold in the
market place to execute those who opposed their intentions, twice submitted the abbey to
veritable siege, and at one time even made it recognise the status of free citizens. But when
Edward III became secure in his possession of the throne he ordered a sheriff to intervene
on the abbot's behalf, and restored his ancient power.[3]

During the long reign of that king (1327-1377) the inhabitants of St. Albans were again
on many occasions inclined to revolt, but they were soon restrained by the iron hand of
their new abbot, Thomas de la Mare. Thomas de la Mare was a man of a lively and
distinguished bearing, respected for his virtues, on terms of close friendship with the king
who made him a member of his Privy Council, and esteemed both by the Black Prince and
by Jean le Bon, who relieved the tedium of his captivity by accepting the abbot's hospitality
at St. Albans.[4] He dedicated his long years as abbot to re-establishing, defending and
increasing the authority and the rights of the abbey, extending its domains, encroaching
upon other properties and rights for the benefit of his house, resisting the encroachments
of others, engaging in litigation, fighting and winning. "No adversary", said H. T. Riley in
his introduction to *Gesta Abbatum Monasterii Sancti Albani,* "was of too exalted a
condition, or of a status too humble, for Abbot Thomas to lose the opportunity, if fairly
offered, of testing with him his legal rights; from kings, princes and archbishops to serfs

and bondmen, from earls, countesses, and ladies of high estate, down to little prioresses and retail dealers in London. To few of the men of those days might one apply more aptly this quotation from Genesis — "His hand was against every man, and every man's hand against him".[5] As for his tenants, he employed towards them an implacable severity, sometimes excessive: after a quarrel with a certain John Chilterne he seized, to avenge himself, fifteen beasts from his flock and let them die of hunger.[6] Such acts were not calculated to earn him popular sympathy; the hatred which had exploded in 1274, 1314 and 1326 persisted, and grew stronger with repression. "When the people of St. Albans stayed quiet", said the chronicler, "it was not bad feelings towards their lords which they lacked, but only the boldness to commit a crime."[7] That boldness the example of the peasants of Essex and Kent gave them: they seized the opportunity when it came.

The crisis broke during the evening of the Feast of the Consecration. Towards midnight, on the night of 13-14 June, the abbot was warned that some people of Barnet had come in haste to St. Albans, bringing a message from the rebels in London: they urged the people of these two localities to rise up without delay, arm themselves and join them, threatening — should they refuse — that twenty-thousand men would come to burn their towns and compel them to revolt by force. Did this message really come from London, or had the people of St. Albans invented it for the sake of their cause, in order to justify to the eyes of a suspicious and implacable lord their departure for the capital? The abbot, later, seems to suggest as much: "They came", he said, "apparently with good intentions but in fact with wickedness and deceit".[8] If this was only a strategem it was a clever one, for the abbot, dreading the arrival of the rebels and their accompanying marauders, recommended to his tenants that they should go to London, "to investigate and spy out their intentions, to negotiate with them and prevent them from coming to St. Albans or the surrounding countryside".[9] He even added to their numbers some of the domestic staff of the monastery and some squires from his own household. Thus, in effect, he gave them a guarantee of tolerance and impunity.

Reassured in this way as to the future, they began to leave at one o'clock in a large body.[10] They passed through Barnet, where their band was swollen by new recruits, and then marched straight to London. That was on the morning of Friday, 14 June — not 13 June as Froissart mistakenly said. The acknowledged leader of this band was a certain William Grindecob, or Gryndecobbe. He had been raised and fed in the monastery, which had been unable, it seems, to inspire in him lively sentiments of filial piety. It seems too that he had no very high degree of family loyalty, for many of his relatives were monks in the abbey.[12] It was not the first time he had been trouble with his former masters: on one occasion when two monks had been sent into the town to survey certain of the abbey's properties, William Grindecob had thrown himself upon them, struck them, and prevented them from doing their work. For this he incurred a public sentence of excommunication, and shortly afterwards had to come, stripped of his clothes, to do penance in front of the convent. This humiliation was not calculated to reconcile him to the abbey authorities: from the outset of the revolt he was to be found at the head of the malcontents, and he remained their leader until the end — till the anxious days of the repression — without regrets, without weakening, with a single-minded obstinacy which was not without a certain grandeur.[13]

As they approached London, at Highbury, the Hertfordshire rebels met a band from Essex, under the leadership of Jack Straw, who had looted and burned the manor which the Prior of the Hospitallers of St.John had had built there. Without hesitation, the people of St. Albans allied themselves with Jack Straw, who, following the practice of the rebels of Kent and London, made them take an oath of obedience to the king and to the people.[14] Having by this oath demonstrated their solidarity with the general mob of rebels, they entered London[15] where they went into a church and took counsel.

The opportunity had come to realise the ambitions they had always nurtured in secret — to enlarge their rights to graze, to fish and to hunt, to make hand querns, to free their town from the dominance of the monastery. But how could they impose their wishes on the abbey? On that point views were divided: some proposed to solicit the aid of Wat Tyler, whom they considered the most powerful man in the kingdom, in order to return in force to St. Albans; others thought it safer to address themselves to the king and to demand of him a sealed letter ordering the abbot to give them satisfaction. They decided that each of these courses was sound, and they prepared to act on them both. First they took themselves to Richard. In what manner and by what means were the rebels of St. Albans able to approach the king? The chroniclers do not say. Probably it was in the field at Mile End, where the serfs of Essex at about the same time obliged Richard to grant their freedom. William Grindecob spoke in the name of his companions: he set out their grievances, and begged the king to redress them, and to obtain the letter that he solicited he knelt six times before the young monarch.

After the king of the nation they addressed themselves to the king of the rebels. This was a less delicate and less intimidating step. It was again Grindecob who explained to Wat Tyler their common complaints. The poor tiler of Maidstone replied grandly that he would go with twenty thousand men if necessary, to shave the beard of the abbot and of the monks — that is to say, added one of the monks naively, to cut off their heads. It was the response of a boastful demagogue, puffed up by his own glittering success, and having lost all touch with reality. But what he added deserves to be noted: he promised them his help on the express condition that they would pledge to him their unconditional obedience; then he drew up for them a complete plan of campaign, laying down how they should conduct themselves on their return to St. Albans, and made them swear to do everything that he had ordered, *quod nihil praeterirent intactum de ejus jussionibus et doctrina.* Here is further evidence of the strength of the political character of Wat Tyler, the concept of discipline at the heart of the revolt. His actual instructions are without interest, but it is important to recognise that it was he who was always giving the orders, he who was organising the disturbances.[16]

There was no longer any doubt about the intentions of the insurgents of St. Albans. They had gone to London not to prevent the ravaging bands from reaching St. Albans, but to secure a double alliance in the struggle which they were going to sustain against their enemy of the past and of the morrow: the monastery. Those people trusted by the abbey — the servants and esquires whom Thomas de la Mare had added to the departing band — had very soon realised the views of their companions, and fearing that they would be accused of complicity, upon arrival at Barnet they had sought out the Earl of Warwick, then passing through that town. They confided to him their fears, and obtained a promise that he would bear witness to their good faith.[17] They accompanied the band to London, but there they parted from it and, after the bloody events of 14 June, returned as quickly as possible to St. Albans.

One of them, the first to arrive at the monastery thanks to the swift pace of his horse, announced to the monks that the Chancellor, the Treasurer and many others had been massacred, that the insurgents were striking down without pity anybody to whom they had taken a dislike, that the prior would be put to death and that the other monks would run great risks if they awaited the return of the rebels. Without waiting for a second warning, the prior immediately took flight, followed by three monks, two lay brothers, some of the servants of the house, and a certain number of advisers and lawyers — anxious no doubt to avoid sharing the fate of the men of law in Kent and in London. These poor frightened people got away by whatever means they could, some on horseback, others on foot, believing that however dangerous their journey it must not stop till they reached the daughter house at Tynemouth in Northumberland.[18] This was perhaps excessively prudent, for to do justice to the rebels of St. Albans, even though passion blinded them and made them resort to violence, they were always too scrupulous — or timid — to shed the blood of holy men.

The prior and the other fugitives had just made their escape when the first of the rebels entered the town. Their troop had split up in London: some stayed there to wait for the letter which the king had promised; the others, in more of a hurry to pay off their grudges and achieve their desires, had immediately taken the road back to the monastery.[19] William Grindecob and one of his principal companions, William Cadingdone, went ahead even of this first band in order to organise the revolt in St. Albans. When the main body of rebels entered the town after them, they announced that the way had been prepared for them to achieve their freedom. Without losing a minute, it was decided to break down the enclosures and the wooden gates which the abbey reserved for its own use, and to demolish a house in the town which belonged to the monastery, the house of the sub-cellerer. No sooner said than done: the rebels went off in a body to the places indicated, preceded by a banner bearing the royal arms which a painter called Thomas had prepared for use in such a situation, carried by a certain John Dene.[20] The fences were shattered, the gates smashed, and the house was demolished. By then it was evening, and silence fell on St. Albans.[21]

Such was the first day of the revolt in this town. Having left before dawn for London, the rebels had taken counsel together, had seen the king and Wat Tyler, had returned and had attacked the property of the abbey. Considering that St. Albans is twenty-two miles from the capital as the crow flies one is amazed at the speed and energy which they deployed. That first day had been well used: those which were to follow were also unlikely to be wasted, and the abbot had some reason to fear such implacable enemies. Certain of the rebels, indeed, had expressed alarming intentions: one of them, Gilbert Taylor, had declared that "if a single rebel was punished by death they would burn down the manors of the abbey and pull down the monastery itself"; and another, John Wayt, more violent still, had said that "he would only be satisfied when they had destroyed all the manors of the abbot and half the abbey".[22]

On Saturday, 15 June, Grindecob and the other leaders resumed their work. From dawn, these "igniters of evil", in the shocked words of the chronicler, had proclaimed throughout the town that each inhabitant who was able-bodied and could carry arms should go to a place called Falconwood.* Those who failed to do so would be punished by death and their dwellings razed to the ground. Everyone, from choice or under duress, came to the rendezvous and a great crowd took counsel together. They decided to continue the war against enclosures and gates, and to destroy them in all the domains of the abbot — in his forests, in his woods, in his warrens. The rebels then over-ran the environs of the town, ravaging in all directions, everywhere breaking down gates and enclosures, obvious and hateful signs of the privileges of the abbey. They no doubt reckoned, somewhat naively, that getting rid of the barriers would assure for themselves users' rights over the property which they had served to enclose. Not content with attacking things, they laid blame on certain persons, and tried to run to earth Robert atte Chamber, forester to the abbot. Being unable to lay hands on his person, they later tore down his house.[23]

When they had achieved these simple successes they returned to St. Albans where they found new recruits. In answer to their call a crowd of peasants from nearby villages had come to support them. In consequence, "they had an exaggerated view of themselves, being strengthened to no small degree, and their spirits were raised up", said the chronicler.[24] They exchanged oaths of fidelity, and put one another in seizin — that is to say, in legal possession of the fields, warrens and woods which belonged to the abbey. Then, having brought in from the countryside a rabbit which — frightened no doubt by the unaccustomed crowd — had allowed itself to be taken alive, they suspended it on high from a lance, carrying it ceremoniously in front of them and fixing it on the St. Albans pillory as a symbol of their new conquest, the freedom of warrens and of hunting.[25] That done, they marched on the abbey. It may seem that they should have begun there; but what concessions could they expect from the abbot so long as the letter promised by Richard II had not arrived? While waiting, they had at least passed the time to some advantage.

The crowd approached the abbey "ove graunt noyse et cry, et ove baners displaiez et pennuz". Thomas de la Mare, fully informed of the rebels' intentions by some of his tenants "whose hearts had been touched by God", considered it necessary to give way, and opened the gates. They went in, and ordered the gate-keeper to let them into the prison, where they released the prisoners. They set all at liberty except one, whom they submitted to further interrogation, found guilty, condemned to death, and executed. Then, in a body, "with the diabolical cries which they had found so stimulating in London at the murder of the Archbishop", they went off with the intention of fixing the head of their victim on top of the pillory.[26]

It is not irrelevant to observe at this point that in all counties where revolution raged — in Kent, in London, in Norfolk, as well as in Hertfordshire — the rebels attacked prisons.

* Falconwood (or Faunton Wood) is on the south-east side of St. Albans in the vicinity of Cunningham Hill, between London Road and Cell Barnes Lane.

That is one of the characteristic features of this revolt. It is not difficult to understand: first, the prison was the cursed place where one paid the slow penalty for having broken the rules; perhaps certain rebels with long memories — like Grindecob, for example — had personal reasons for ordering this action against the lord's dungeons. But there was more to it than that: to empty the prisons was not just to release some poor captives and take vengeance for past injuries; it also gave notice of a new regime where laws would be fair, where judgments would be made on different principles. It was for the rebels a means of declaring their sovereignty. And it was only to be expected that in putting such ideas into practice they would submit the prisoners to a new judgment, condemning one to death while acquitting his companions.

The rebels who had remained the previous night in London trickled back to St. Albans during the day and increased the number of insurgents in the town.[27] About nine o'clock in the morning, just as the prisoners from the abbey had been set at liberty, a group arrived preceded by a standard bearing the arms of St. George, "following the practice of the murderers of London", as the chronicler put it. The leader of this group was Richard de Wallingford, one of the chief of the St. Albans rebels, who bore the letter from the king. At the news of his approach the rebels went into the fields to meet him. He got down from his horse, stuck the standard in the ground, and ordered all the people to gather round him as in times of war. After talking to them for some time, he told them to wait there while he ascertained the abbot's intentions. He entered the church with several of the leading rebels, and ordered Thomas de la Mare to come to the same place in order to reply to the people.[28]

Although the choice of this meeting place may seem surprising to us today, it was in accordance with the usual practice of the middle ages, when the church did not serve only for religious celebrations. It was often the only stone building of the village, always the warmest and lightest, and many would stop there to transact business; goods might be stored there.[29] Nothing was more natural than to have summoned Thomas de la Mare thither, instead of talking in the open air amidst the crowd of rebels.

"The abbot", the chronicler tell us, "was resolved to die in defence of the privileges of the monastery, rather than agree to anything that was prejudicial to his house. But he was moved by the prayers, the warnings and the assurances of his monks, who represented to him how useless his death would be to the monastery. Even though he had quite decided to die, he was won over by their arguments and went down to meet the rebels." This attitude is little in accord with the energetic and belligerent character of Thomas de la Mare, but if correctly recorded it was the action of a wise man to change his mind.

When the abbot entered the church, Richard de Wallingford briefly saluted him, and handed him the letter which according to the chronicler he had "extorted" from the king. This letter contained the following message:

"Very dear in God.

At the petition of our beloved lieges of the town of St. Albans, we do will and command that certain charters, being in your keeping, made by our progenitor, King Henry, unto the burgesses and good folks of the said town, of common, and of pasture, and of piscary, and of certain other advantages, expressed in the same charters, as they say, you do cause to be delivered unto the said burgesses and good folks, the which law and right require; that so they may have no ground for making plaint from henceforth unto us for such reason.

Given under our signet at London, the fifteenth day of June, in the fourth year of our reign".[30]

The abbot received and read this document "with the respect that was due to the king", but that did not prevent him from refusing every concession, saying that these matters had been decided once and for all and that the relevant records of the agreements were preserved in the official rolls at Westminster. Consequently, according to the universally respected law of the land, the inhabitants had no right to what they were demanding.

Richard de Wallingford, imbued with the same ideas which had caused the rebels to attack the abbey prison, replied that the old laws had lapsed, that they had no respect for them, and that they would listen to no arguments of that kind. He exhorted the abbot not to try the patience of the mob, who would only be quietened by receiving full satisfaction of their demands.

Thomas de la Mare, unwilling to give way, looked for other arguments; but Richard threatened him with the fury of his companions, who were resolved, if they were kept waiting for a reply, to call for twenty thousand men from Wat Tyler to raze the monastery to the ground. The abbot tried to appeal to reasons of sentiment: he reminded them that he had been abbot for many years and that he had never caused them any harm; whenever they had been in distress he had tried to help them; they were attacking in him a friend, and the gentlest of masters. They replied that they knew all about his merits, but that at that moment the only course open to him was to accede to their demands. The abbot could only submit.[31] He granted them everything they wanted, as he explained later in his petition to the king, "in order to avoid the death of his monks and to turn aside the great malice which they felt towards the said abbey".[32]

Immediately the villeins particularised their demands: they wanted the charters of liberties; Thomas de la Mare promised that they should have them. Their predecessors had given various undertakings to the abbey under threat of having to pay a fine of three thousand marks; they wanted to be freed from the obligations registered in that agreement. Finally, criticising the justice of the abbey in regard to the practice of imprisonment, they demanded a share in responsibility for administering justice. They were given all the documents for which they asked, and carried them off, made a heap of them in the open space near the cross, and set fire to them.[33]

Thomas de la Mare was also obliged to humiliate himself in front of them:

"On top of everything", he said later in his petition to the king, "they would only undertake to keep the peace if the abbot himself would go outside the church and beg the forgiveness of the mob, which he did".[34] But this energetic and resourceful man was ready to turn the situation to account: being unable to make any impression on the leaders, he tried to win over the crowd. Profiting from the humiliating ceremony which brought him into unwilling contact with them, he showed them a charter of the liberties which their forefathers had extorted from one of his predecessors, and which a short time afterwards had been, with their full agreement, annulled before the king's court. He hoped that the memory of that unhappy attempt would make them pause and reflect. But rebels seldom learn from the lessons of history. They expect to be more fortunate than their predecessors. Whatever they are able to extract they hope to be able to keep.[35]

They insistently demanded an old charter of St. Albans, conveying freedom to the serfs, and decorated they said with two coloured majuscules, one of gold, the other of blue.[36] What was this famous enactment? Was it the charter of King Henry I referred to in the king's letter? Was it the supposed charter of ancient Offa? Rebels at St. Albans had always particularly cherished the memory of that ancient sovereign: according to one story it was he who had brought people together at this place — artisans, craftsmen, smiths, joiners, masons — to build the monastery, and had granted to them a series of rights and privileges later suppressed by the abbots and the monks. The people of St. Albans had invoked his authority in the course of earlier revolts, and expressed their wish to return to the time of the good king Offa.[37]

This enactment, whose appearance the rebels described, the abbot had never seen nor heard of. But it was dangerous to deny them anything they demanded. Thomas de la Mare, at a loss what to do, asked for a truce on the pretext of searching particularly for this charter which could not be found, promising if he discovered it to hand it over without fail at three o'clock: if they would come back then, they would be satisfied.[38] Thus was a short respite gained.

The author of *Historia Anglicana* described the monks trying in vain to regain their strength by eating: "It did them no good, for they were eating the bread of sorrow, and their drink mingled with their tears. Life and death were in the hands of the peasants whom they could not control, and whom they could not forgive".[39] This was in fact only a truce, and the struggle was about to be resumed, mercilessly by the victors, hopelessly by the vanquished.

Already the rebels had attacked the abbey buildings. The monastery parlour[40] was paved with stone slabs, whose origin was dear to the hearts of the people of St. Albans: they were the millstones which they themselves had formerly used when they were allowed, in spite of the privileges accorded to the abbey, to set up hand querns in their homes. After a long drawn out legal wrangle the monks had won the right to confiscate them, and had placed them in this position "as a reminder of the wrong and injury which they had done to the abbey". After the meeting with the abbot, one group obtained entry to this parlour, prised up the stones, carried them outside, smashed them and distributed the pieces among the rebels, this time as a souvenir of the defeat of the monastery.[41]

But the respite drew to a close: at the appointed hour an immense crowd — according to the chronicler — gathered before the abbey and all the rebels with one voice cried out that if the authorities did not hand over to them the charters they demanded they would pull down the great gate. The ever resourceful abbot, however, had not wasted the respite he had gained, but had drawn up a new charter of liberties. He offered it to them, promising that it would be properly validated if it met with their approval. It goes without saying that they were not satisfied. They demanded that Thomas de la Mare should send to them a clerk, armed with ink and parchment, who would write at their dictation; the abbot had only to set his seal on the statement which they would draft. He was obliged to accept their conditions: at the orders of his subjects he sent the ink, the parchment, and the secretary. One can imagine this unfortunate clerk writing down a 'charter of freedom' at the dictation of a multitude of over-excited individuals, undisciplined, gesticulating, calling out conflicting advice. No doubt they were at some pains to ensure that their intentions were correctly recorded, but when the statement composed in this way had been drawn up and sealed they were still not satisfied, and reverted with renewed ardour to demanding with a great outcry the old charter with gold and blue majuscules.[42]

The abbot, his spirit much cast down, was unable to give them that supreme satisfaction, and despaired of convincing them of his good faith. He sent to them honest and highly regarded squires, to promise that on the following day, Sunday, he would celebrate mass in their presence and would swear on the holy sacrament, as would all his monks, that they did not knowingly retain the charter which was claimed. But the rebels being naturally distrustful, refused to be convinced by the most solemn oaths. In response to the squires they said that either they would have the missing charter which they claimed, or they would set fire to the monastery. The abbot, unwilling to admit defeat, sent back the squires to them to explain that they were demanding the impossible, and to propose to them the following arrangement: that they themselves should re-create the ancient charter of their dreams, making it up in accordance with their recollections or as they understood it to have been; for his part, he undertook in advance to sign it and seal it with the seal of the abbey. There could not be a more satisfactory settlement.

This gesture was not without effect. Some of the rebels — the more moderate or the more weary — urged that they should give the monks a further extension of the truce until nine o'clock on the following day; but the majority, more implacable, were for continuing to press their demands. The abbot, realising that hunger and thirst were bad counsellors and that the rebels would be less dangerous fed than fasting, arranged for the distribution of bread and beer at the abbey gates. This was the most persuasive response he could possibly have made, the one most likely to be listened to. It calmed them down. It was no longer impossible to reason with them, and that responsibility was undertaken by one of the leading inhabitants of the city. Noting that there were among the rebels beseiging the monastery a good number of villagers from the surrounding countryside, he went to them and reproached them with some shrewdness for seeking to take away from the townspeople of St. Albans the dangerous honour of getting the better of the abbey; and he proposed that they should withdraw and join the rebels who were operating in the town.[43]

This advice, which they thought came from one of their own people, seemed to them to be sound, and they dropped out, going back into the town, and devoted the rest of the day, which had begun so well, to wreaking their vengeance on the employees of the monastery. The abbot had promised to atone for any misdeeds which these servants had committed, and to dismiss the culprits from his service; but the rebels seem not to have had much confidence in the promises of Thomas de la Mare and intended to exact justice themselves. They went to the dwellings of Richard Scryvein, Robert atte Chamber, John Clerk and Simon Lymbrennere [Limeburner], broke down the walls and burned whatever they found inside. Why had they chosen these four, among all the officers of the abbey, as scapegoats? Without doubt because their profession was particularly odious: Robert atte Chamber was the forest warden of the monastery, responsible for protecting the monks' right of warren; Richard Scryvein and John Clerk were, as their names indicate, two of those hated secretaries whose job it was to represent authority, who had drawn up the titles and who were custodians of the registers of the abbot's seignorial power, and upon whose word the abbot oppressed his tenants and punished those who did not meet his demands. This, in another form, was 'the hatred of the inkwell' which had been evident also in Kent and in London. Only in the case of Simon Lymbrennere is the relevance of his trade not clear.[44]

As in the counties to the south, the rebels regarded the king as their ally against their lords: John Eccleshale, who is recorded in the judicial rolls as having been the first to rise in St. Albans and who led the group which laid waste these houses, ordered them to do this 'in the name of the king'.[45] This naive loyalty should perhaps be recognised as one of the most general and most interesting features of the revolt of 1381.

The satisfactions to be gained in this way were only shortlived. The real focus of the rising, that which had to be overcome, was not the servants or employees of the abbey, but the abbey itself. Thomas de la Mare had given the rebels only promises; it was necessary, by concentrating their forces, to compel him to authorise unreservedly, and without any possibility of later renunciation, the concessions which they had extorted. So, as evening approached, the rebels gathered in the market place and there, beneath their standard, they formally proclaimed that all men of the neighbourhood should come and join with them in arms once more, "to help to maintain the rights of the king and the people." Anyone, they added, who had a debt owing from the abbey should come on the morrow to claim what was due to him. The townspeople of St. Albans should strive to satisfy themselves, from the goods of the monastery, so far as those goods would suffice.[46]

This proclamation was cleverly drafted. By addressing themselves to the peasants' instinctive cupidity they made the revolution seem more attractive, and might hope to increase their numbers; by disposing in such a high-handed way of the goods of the monastery they flaunted their own new sovereignty.

Their appeal brought results: you might even say it was anticipated. At the very moment when it was issued a man entered the abbey armed from top to toe, a sword in one hand and a shield in the other, claimed 100 marks in a loud voice, and threatened that if he was refused he would set fire to the grange of St. Peter and the manor of Kingsbury, just outside the town. He was the former tenant of the manor, who had assumed the apparel of a man at arms. He owed money to the monastery, and having a healthy respect for the rigour of the law had thought it wise to run away. But during his forced absence — dedicated, he said, to getting together the money which he owed — he had had ample time to reflect. All things considered, he owed nothing to the abbey. On the contrary, he was entitled to an indemnity of 100 marks as compensation for the inconvenience he had been caused through being obliged to leave his manor. At last the time of justice had come! But it was not in the nature of Thomas de la Mare to give way without a struggle. They bargained, and — said the chronicler — moved by the prayers addressed to him, the citizen settled for twenty pounds — that is to say, 30 marks — and went away satisfied.[47]

On that same day there were other scenes of this kind, and the drama of the revolt was lightened by several amusing incidents. But the majority of the rebels were in deadly earnest, believing that the hour of regeneration was at hand, and played their parts seriously, even tragically. They had no illusions about the attitude of the abbot. They knew that that brave and obstinate man would use every means to escape the demands of his enemies. They were afraid, therefore, that he would take advantage of darkness to obtain armed reinforcements, remembering similar situations in the past when force had been used to overcome the claims of their fathers. So, in the proclamation they had issued in the market place, they had ordered that the monastery should be surrounded by a chain of sentries keeping close watch on all exit routes, so that no monk should be able to get out of the abbey or return to it. If any monk should fall into their hands they were either to cut off his head or keep him under close guard until the morning. More than 100 persons, claims the chronicler, answered the call and took a share during the night in the blockade of the monastery.[48]

So ended the second day of the revolt in St. Albans. In a few hours the rebels had broken down the fences of woods and warrens, beseiged the prison, bested the abbot in a desperate face-to-face encounter, wrenched the paving from the floor of the parlour, sacked several houses, and ensured by their proclamations the spread of the revolt. There was no doubt either that it would continue, or that the next day the rebels would act with equal determination: they had not said their last word.

The monks, who foresaw this, passed a terrible night. What could they do, more than on the previous evening to satisfy the rebels? They could not sleep without dreaming of the massacres in Kent and in London, of which grim tales had reached them. "Disheartened", said Walsingham, "the majority were of a mind to flee".

But Sunday, which seemed bound to witness their ruin, brought instead their salvation. At daybreak it became known at St. Albans that Wat Tyler had been killed, and that the citizens of London had risen up to give chase to the rebels; and there had arrived a messenger from the king, who proclaimed peace in the name of the sovereign, ordering that all should respect it on pain of forfeiting life and limb. Moreover, this messenger brought to the abbot a letter of protection, in the following terms:

"Richard, by the grace of God king of England and of France and Lord of Ireland, to all our lieges and commons of the County of Hertford, and of all other Counties adjoining and near thereto. We do pray you, charge, and command, the most strictly that we may, and upon the faith and allegiance which unto us you owe, that you do not, nor suffer to be done, so far as in you lies, any grievance, damage, or molestation whatsoever, in body or goods, in any manner whatsoever, unto our very dear in God, the Abbot of Saint Albans, or unto our house and Monastery of the said place, which is of our patronage, or unto any of the people, monks or others, or unto any of the goods, within the said monastery, and the enclosure thereof, and in any other places whatsoever of the said Abbey being, or unto it and its appurtenances, for if the said Abbot, or any of his people, has offended as towards you, we ourselves will make him give redress for the same, and make amends, as right shall demand. And this our command take so to heart, that it may behove us to congratulate you upon all the love

96

and loyalty that unto us you bear.

"Given under our great seal at our City of London, the fifteenth day of June, the fourth year of our reign".[49]

So this decree bore the same date as the other, which the rebels had extorted from the king for their own ends. What an unexpected transformation in a few hours!

The chronicler, recalling this very happy news, could not forbear to strike up a song of joy: "Then", he said, "did this Sunday shine forth, when divine consolation began to smile upon the frightened and the oppressed. The impudence of the villeins was humbled, and the pride of yesterday crumbled today in a way that could not have been dreamed of".[50]

The death of Wat Tyler, though it did not affect them materially, was a severe blow to the morale of the rebels at St. Albans. Wat Tyler was the overall leader of the rising, whose alliance they had proudly sought, of whose imminent arrival to take vengeance they had given warning, and who had inspired all the more confidence through being an unknown and shadowy figure. But however great were the consequences of this event, it had no immediate effect at St. Albans. The determination of the rebels was at first unaffected by the news: since the previous evening their numbers had been swelled by a crowd of new supporters as a result of their rallying call to the surrounding countryside. They no doubt regarded themselves as a force of considerable strength, and in spite of the King's decree they returned at the appointed hour in quest of the documents to which they had laid claim the day before.

The chronicler insists that they behaved with the utmost moderation, "adopting a reasonable tone". They asked only for a charter setting out their rights, promising if they obtained it that there would be permanent peace between the town and the monastery. The abbot and his monks, delighted at the way things had turned out, put up no further struggle. They were now reassured about the future, and they waited for the rising to peter out. Two knights, Thomas Percy and Hugh Segrave, senseschal of the king, advised Thomas de la Mare to agree to anything, guaranteeing that the monastery would not suffer in consequence. The abbot therefore received the principal rebels, put a clerk at their disposal, and allowed them to draft the so much desired charter. Then he signed it and sealed it, without any reservation.*

That charter, dated 16 June, is very long but can be briefly summarised: the abbot acknowledged, for all citizens of St. Albans, first, an absolute right of passage, of pasture, and of hunting over certain large areas, clearly defined; second, a right of fishing in certain waters; third, he allowed each person to set up a hand mill, in his house or elsewhere; fourth, he granted to the town the right to self-government, without interference from the abbey bailiff.[51]

It is possible, with the help of this charter and other documents, to understand something of what was in the minds of the rebels. Note the order in which the concessions, set down by the rebels themselves, were placed: the last, political in nature, which today would be the most important, is mentioned in only three lines at the end of the deed; the preceding clause, dealing with mills and of mainly social significance, is somewhat more detailed. But all the emphasis in the charter, all the elaboration, is lavished on the first

* The text of the charter, is published on pages 123/4.

clauses. The mere order may not seem to us important, and we have some difficulty in understanding why anyone should rise up in revolt merely to extort a right to hunt or to fish. The people of the Middle Ages saw things differently, and with good reason. For country people today hunting and fishing are little more than sport, but they were important sources of food at a time when in winter there was only dried or salted meat to eat, since the great majority of cattle were killed in the autumn for lack of winter forage. Poaching, too, a common offence at all times, was particularly rife in the Middle Ages when hunting was strictly reserved for the upper classes: consequently it was subject to exceptionally heavy penalties, and the right of warren remained the most detested of all the so-called feudal rights.

The charter of freedom, written at the dictation of the rebels, exactly as they wanted it, without any modification, is in this regard particularly illuminating: the first freedom that they claimed was to be able to hunt or fish as they wished. At the same time they extended their right to pasture, to provide better feed for their cattle. As for self-government, although that was a right which they also sought it was only a secondary consideration.

All that was lacking, to give them complete satisfaction, was the handing over to them of the old charter containing the illuminated letters which they remembered so well. That old charter, missing on Saturday, could still not be found on Sunday. Happily for the monks, the rebels were less bold than on the previous day, and negotiation was possible. The abbot undertook, if he found the required document, to hand it over to the townspeople of St. Albans before 25 March 1382. If he was not able to find it an oath, taken on the gospels by himself and the twelve oldest monks of the monastery, would vouch for his sincerity. In that event, in place of the charter, the townspeople would be able within the same period to demand another document confirming their ancient freedoms, and to insert new clauses in the charter conceded on 16 June. To set the seal on these agreements, the abbot undertook in advance that should he fail to abide by them he should pay to his subjects the sum of £1,000, payable on 25 March 1382.[52]

It remained only for the rebels to take one final but indispensable precaution: to ensure their own immunity by means of an amnesty. So Thomas de la Mare was required to authorise a third document, called a 'quit-claim', granting a general pardon. By this, the abbot renounced all punitive action against the people of St. Albans "from the beginning of the world until the present day". Only process for the recovery of debts was excluded from this undertaking.[53]

These three documents were drawn up at the dictation of the rebels, who strolled round the monastery, said Walsingham, "not like servants but like masters", and each was validated in their presence. "Then", said the chronicler, "a marvellous thing happened: just as the charter of the townspeople's freedom was being sealed, and with all the requisite care and ceremony the common seal (a very old seal bearing a representation of St. Alban, the glorious proto-martyr of the Britons) had been applied to the wax, it proved impossible at three attempts to lift it off or wrench it away, clearly a sign that the martyr did not want them as overlords, but wanted them to be ruled as before".[54] The poor secretaries of the seal, very nervous at doing this unaccustomed job in the midst of a crowd which did not cease to scare them, had no doubt omitted some essential precaution to prevent the wax from adhering to the seal!

Once in possession of their charters the representatives of the rebels went off in high spirits. They re-assembled at the foot of the cross and there, in front of the whole assembled crowd, they read out the deeds which they had wrested from the abbot. After the concessions granted by Thomas de la Mare, they told them about those of Richard II: the king, at the insistence of the rebels of Essex and following the encounter at Mile End, had two days before freed all the serfs in the kingdom, and granted to the insurgents a free pardon, by letters patent granted in council.[55] Some of the rebels had brought back to St. Albans a copy of the King's letter, addressed to all inhabitants of the county of Hertford: and they read it out in front of the crowd. It is easy to imagine the emotions with which this was received. Not that the question of serfdom had been a big issue in that area: the townspeople had not risen up for that reason. But the royal amnesty, on top of the abbot's pardon, was their supreme assurance for the future. It is true that the amnesty applied only to acts committed before 14 June; but the leaders of the revolt had been careful to keep quiet about the royal letters patents until after the complete capitulation of the abbot, hoping that by means of this deception he would pardon all misdemeanours committed before the terms of the royal pardon were known.[56]

So the insurrection at St. Albans was brought to an end. To demonstrate this, and to give clear proof of their moderation, the rebels proclaimed, in their own name, the charter of protection granted to the monks by the king. Thus, like truly benevolent princes, they pardoned the abbey for the ills they had done to it![57] Then, light of heart, they dispersed and spread round the town, shouting, and followed by carts full of bread and beer; and from the vantage point of each boundary stone they passed it round and drank freely.[58] And so this revolt, after three days of violence, ended amid public rejoicing.

1. The abbot recalled this with pride in his petition to the king, after the rising. See *Rotuli Parliamentorum*, III, 129a, no. 10.

2. *De diversis ordinationibus praedicti abbatis, maneria et temporalia monasterii S.Albani concernentibus* (Ordonnances de Roger de Norton, 24th abbot of St. Albans, 1260-1290), in *Gesta*, I, 453 et seq.

3. *Gesta*, III, introduction by H. T. Riley, p.xxxvii-xxxix, l-lii. [Cf.p.xl-xli, a strange story about an attempt by the inhabitants, in the time of Edward II, to throw discredit on the morals of the monks.]

4. *Gesta*, III, p.lxiii-lxiv.

5. *Ibid.* p.x. Cf. *ibid*, p.lxviii, and Edward Levien, 'On popular tumults at St. Albans in the reign of Richard II', in the *Journal of the British Archaeological Association*, xxvi, p. 37, 39. [M. Levien in this paper made a study of the troubles of 1381, but he was not aware of certain very important records and in addition his sketch lacks order and clarity.]

6. *Gesta*, III, Intro., p.lxiv-lxv.

7. "Itaque demonstraverunt palam tempore tranquillitatis non eis malitiam adversus dominos suos, sed audaciam operandi nequitiam, defuisse." (*Hist Anglic*, II, append. B, p. 395. The same text is in *Gesta*, III, 329).

8. *Gesta*, III, 289. This petition, included in the *Gesta* under the title of "Gravamina per tenentes monasterii Sancti Albani eidem abbati violenter illata", was addressed to the king and his council a few days after the revolt. It is a particularly important document on that account.

9. *Ibid.*

10. "Bien entour cynk centz". (*Ibid*, p. 290).

11. "Early on Friday". (Petition of the abbot: *Gesta*, III, 290). Froissart (Édition Luce and Raynaud, X, 100, 101, 114), sets these events in the county of *Stafford*; he apparently confused Stafford and Hertford. There was no revolt in the county of Stafford.

12. *Chron. Angl.*, p. 300. The same text is in *Hist. Anglic.*, I, 468, and in *Gesta*, III, 300. [I found among the papers collected by Andre Réville a letter patent of Richard II which he had analysed thus: "1384, 19 March. The King grants to Roger Cokerell, chaplain, seven sous of rent annually, to be collected at St. Albans, having belonged formerly to William Grindecob who was condemned to death following the rising, and also the reversion of two small dwellings with their outhouses, in the possession of Joan, widow of the said William". *Patent 7, Ric. II, part 2, membr.1.*]

13. *Gesta*, III, 369.

14. And not 'to the king and to the commons', the mistaken reading usually adopted. The Latin word *communes* should here be understood to mean not the commons, but the 'not noble', the masses. *Chron. Angl.*, p. 290. See also *Hist. Anglic.*, I, 458, and *Gesta*, III, 298.

15. M. Stubbs (*Constit. history*, 4th ed., II, 479) says wrongly that the rebels from Hertfordshire camped on the evening of the 13th at Highbury.

16. *Chron. Angl.*, 299-300. Also in *Hist. Anglic.*, I, 467-469, and *Gesta*, III, 298-300.

17. *Gesta*, III, 297-298.

18. *Chron. Angl.*, p. 300-301. Also in *Hist. Anglic.*, I, 469, and *Gesta*, III, 301. See also *Gesta*, III, 287.

19. Petition of the abbot, in *Gesta*, III, 290.

20. ". . . Thomas Payntor de Sancto Albano, die veneris proximo post festum Corporis Christi, anno regis nunc Anglie quarto, depixit quoddam vexillum de armis domini regis, et tradidit illud Johanni Dene ad portandum . . ." (*Coram rege, Mich. 5 Ric. II, m. 26*).

21. *Chron. Angl.*, 301. *Hist. Anglic.*, I, 469-470; also in *Gesta*, III, 301-302. "Johannes Tyler et alii simul cum aliis malefactoribus et pacis domini regis perturbatoribus, die veneris proximo ante festum Nativitatis sancti Johannis Baptiste . . . quandam domum abbatis de Sancto Albano vocatam Le Thwethonerhous, apud villam de Sancto Albano proditorie fregerunt et prosternarunt". (*Coram rege, Mich. 5 Ric. II, m. 27d*). — Cf. *Coram rege, Trinity 5 Ric. II, m. 33 and 33 dorso*. — The date Friday 21 June, which is given by the document somewhat abridged above, is obviously wrong. It must be the previous Friday, 14 June. The other texts agree on this point.

22. ". . . Gilbertus Taillor, de Sancto Albano, die veneris proximo post festum Corporis Christi, surexit proditorie apud Sanctum Albanum, cum comitate iniqua, ut inimicus domini regis, contra dictum dominum regem, contra legianciam suam, et dixit quod si quis homo mortuus fuerit pro sureccione predicta, quod tunc maneria abbatis de Sancto Albano comburarentur et abbatia predicta esset prosternata". — ". . . Johannes Wayt de Sancto Albano surexit die veneris proximo post festum Corporis Christi, anno regni regis nunc Anglie quarto, apud villam de Santo Albano, prodiciose cum comitate ejusdem ville qui surexerunt contra dominum regem ibidem, in prejudicium domini regis et corone sue, contra legianciam suam, et dixit quod nunquam haberent propositum suum, quousque prosternassent omnia maneria abbati Sancti Albani circa abbatiam existencia, et medietatem dicte abbatie". (*Coram rege, Mich. 5 Ric. II, m. 27*).

23. *Hist. Anglic.*, I, 470; also in *Gesta*, III, 302. — *Gesta*, III, 288, 370.

24. *Hist. Anglic.*, I, 471; also in *Gesta*, III, 303. The chronicler with his habitual exaggeration, estimated the number of these new arrivals at 2,000.

25. *Gesta*, III, 303.

26. Petition of the abbot, in *Gesta*, III, 290-291. — *Hist. Anglic.*, I, 471; also in *Gesta*, III, 303-304. — ". . . Quidam Johannes Baron, die sabati proximo post festum Corporis Christi, quendam hominem cujus nomen incognitum est eis, qui in prisona abbatis de Sancto Albano in Sancto Albano detinebatur . . ., extra prisonam illam cepit et decapitavit". (*Coram rege, Easter 5 Ric. II, m. 18*). — Cf. *Coram rege, Mich. 5 Ric. II, m. 27, dorso*.

27. Petition of the abbot: *loc. cit.*, p. 290.

28. *Hist. Anglic.*, I, 472; also in *Gesta*, III, 304-305. — "Johannes Garlek et alii . . ., die sabbati proximo post festum predictum, eodem anno, venerunt de Londoniis cum uno vexillo usque villam de Sancto Albano contra dominum, etc., et contra ligeanciam suam". (*Coram rege, Mich. 5 Ric. II, m. 28. Cf. m. 26 d.*)

29. Rogers. *History of agriculture and prices in England*, I, 59.

30. *Hist. Anglic.*, I, 472-473; also in *Gesta*, III, 305-306. An edited text of the royal letters can also be found in *Hist. Anglic.*

31. *Hist. Anglic.*, I, 473-474; also in *Gesta*, III, 306-308.

32. Petition of the abbot: *Gesta*, III, 291.

33. Petition of the abbot: *loc. cit.*, 291-292. — *Hist. Anglic.*, I, 474; also in *Gesta*, III, 308.

34. Petition of the abbot: *loc. cit.*, 292.

35. *Ibid.*, 292-293.

36. *Ibid.*, 291.

37. *Gesta*, III, 365.

38. *Gesta*, III, 308-309. — *Hist. Anglic.*, I, 474-475.

39. *Hist. Anglic.*, I, 475; also in *Gesta*, III, 309.

40. And not the cloister, as Green said. See J. R. Green, *Short history of the English people.*

41. Petition of the abbot, *loc. cit.*, 293. — *Hist. Anglic.*, I, 475; also in *Gesta*, III, 309.

42. *Hist. Anglic.*, I, 476; also in *Gesta*, III, 310-311.

43. *Hist. Anglic.*, I, 476-477; also in *Gesta*, III, 311-312.

44. *Coram rege, Mich. 5 Ric. II, m. 26, 27 dorso, 28 dorso; Easter 5 Ric. II, m. 18; Trin. 5 Ric. II, m. 23 dorso, 33.* — These outrages were said to have taken place on Saturday, 22 June (*Mich., etc., m. 27 dorso, and Trin., etc., m. 33*). This was obviously a mistake for Saturday, 15 June. Other diplomatic documents and chronicles agree on that point. (Cf. Petition of the abbot, in *Gesta*, III, 295-295; — *Hist. Anglic.*, I, 478; also in *Gesta*, III, 312-313.)

45. ". . . Predictus Johannes Eccleshale fuit primus surrector in villa de Sancto Albano . . . et fecit quasdam proclamaciones in eadem villa, quod homines ejusdem ville surgerent cum ipso, et fuit ductor quorumdam inimicorum et malefactorum ad domos Johannis Clerke, Ricardi Scryveyn et Roberti atte Chambre prosternandum proditorie, et mandavit illis malefactoribus ex parte dicti domini regis prosternandum, die dominica post festum Corporis Christi". (*Coram rege, Trin. 5 Ric. II, m. 33 and 33 dorso*). The date given by this document is also inaccurate.

46. Petition of the abbot: *loc. cit.*, p. 295. — *Hist. Anglic.*, I, 478; also in *Gesta*, III, 313.

47. *Hist. Anglic.*, I, 478-479; also in *Gesta*, III, 313-314.

48. *Hist. Anglic.*, I, 478.

49. *Ibid.*, I, 479-481; also in *Gesta*, III, 314-316.

50. *Hist. Anglic.*, I, 479; also in *Gesta*, III, 315.

51. *Gesta*, III, 317-320. [*Hist. Anglic.*, I, 481-483, differs in many respects: it does not contain even a summary of this charter, which is transcribed fully in the *Gesta*.] Cf. *Annales de Dunstaplia*, p. 417; Knighton, II, 141.

52. *Gesta*, III, 320-322.

53. *Ibid.*, III, 322. (Cf. *ibid.*, p. 288, and *Hist. Anglic.*, I, 482).

54. *Hist. Anglic.*, I, 483; also in *Gesta*, III, 323.

55. Rymer, IV, 126.

56. *Hist. Anglic.*, I, 481-483; also in *Gesta*, III, 317-318, 323-324.

57. *Hist. Anglic.*, I, 483; also in *Gesta*, III, 323-324.

58. *Gesta abbatum*, III, 320.

CHAPTER 2. THE REVOLT OF THE OTHER TENANTS OF THE ABBOT OF ST. ALBANS

The rebels had reached St. Albans on Saturday, 15 June. But the biggest crowd assembled at the abbey from Sunday the 16th till Thursday 20th June. Many of them merely wanted the abbot to acknowledge and adopt the charter of rights which had been granted by the king, but others demanded further concessions.

The inhabitants of St. Albans were not the only ones to take part in the drama which unfolded in their town. The rising, as it spread, aroused many active supporters throughout Hertfordshire, who flocked to join the crowd at St. Albans. Their contribution was far from insignificant.

Right from the start the citizens of St. Albans had acted in concert with those of Watford and Barnet in the south, and they had attracted as many of them as they could during their march on London. From the Friday, when they were on their way back, the news of their exploits spread throughout the countryside and attracted to their cause the sympathies of the surrounding villagers. On the Saturday morning they had ordered by public proclamation all able-bodied men to join them, and in the evening they repeated that call, this time addressing themselves specifically to the people of Hertfordshire. The invitation was heard the more readily because it had to some extent been anticipated: the people in the immediate vicinity of St. Albans were the quickest to respond, and when in the morning the rebels re-entered the town having laid waste the monastery's woods and warrens, they found a great crowd of supporters come in from the countryside, a crowd so impressive that the chronicler, known in other contexts to be given to exaggeration, estimated their number at two-thousand.[1]

A little later, just as the door of the abbey prison had been forced, there arrived at St. Albans a fresh group who had come from the extreme south of the county and even beyond.[2] Then it was the turn of the men of Redbourn and Berkhamsted lying to the west of St. Albans, the latter some ten miles away close to the Buckinghamshire border, and it was before their eyes and with their help that the house of Robert atte Chamber was demolished. Edmund Cook and some others — about 40 in all — say the chronicles, hurried over from Berkhamsted on horseback and stood gloating in front of the house they were destroying until it had been entirely demolished.[3] The next day, Sunday, more supporters from Watford, Rickmansworth and Tring took part in the noisy demonstrations at St. Albans.[4]

Only then did the flood really begin: during the five days from Sunday to Thursday people from a large number of villages streamed into the abbey: Northaw, Sandridge, Tittenhanger, in the St. Albans area; Cashiobury, near Watford; Abbots Langley, in the direction of Berkhamsted; Walden, Norton, Hexton, Caldecote, Shephall, Newnham, Aston, in the country between St. Albans and Hitchin — the whole of the eastern part of the county.[5] The rebels at St. Albans could boast, as did their companions from Redbourn, that their company included representatives from 32 localities, and parliament later attributed the violence of which the abbey had been the victim to its tenants as a whole, "people of the town of St. Albans and others".[6]

102

They all came to the monastery, not only to help the cause of the townspeople, but also in their own interests: taking advantage of the opportunity created by the disturbances they also demanded charters of liberties. Most often they merely asked Thomas de la Mare to apply to their own case the terms granted by the king after the confrontation at Mile End, and the abbot handed over to them an undertaking sealed with his seal and that of the chapter. He granted three charters of this kind on 16 June, eleven the next day, one on Tuesday the 18th and five on Thursday the 20th. After that date he seems to have handed over no more.[7]

But not all of the abbey's tenants were so easily satisfied, and many put forward other claims. Thus, on the Saturday, the people of Redbourn had claimed not only the freeing of serfs and the suppression of liability to forced labour of all kinds, but also additional rights to hunt and to fish. They had taken along with them, according to the chronicler, several noblemen — Edmund Cresey, William Eyle, Thomas Norton and others — and forced them, on pain of death, to speak up on their behalf. Thomas de la Mare replied that he was disposed to grant their freedom on the general lines of the charter granted by the king. As for the other concessions they claimed, he said he would need to discuss them with his council, and he promised only that he would give them on the following Thursday a reply which would satisfy them. But by that date the contingent from Redbourn had already left, carrying with them only one of the abbot's abstracts.[8]

The rebels from Barnet made claims of another kind. The houses in which they lived belonged to the abbey, and it went without saying that their occupancy was subject to the payment of certain dues. They presented themselves at the monastery on 15 June and demanded that there should be handed over to them the volume of the court rolls in which these dues were recorded, boldly announcing their intention of burning it. The abbot, thus warned, decided to play for time, and undertook only to deliver the volume to them within three weeks. Henry Frowik and some of his companions having been given written guarantees of that promise, the Barnet contingent withdrew, carrying at least a document by which Thomas de la Mare confirmed in their favour the freedom granted by the king's letter and recognised their right to sell as they wished their houses and holdings.[9]

The rebels from Rickmansworth obtained on 15 June a charter still more advantageous: the abbot acknowledged them to be free, as in the previous charters, and allowed them also to dispose as they themselves wished of their lands, requiring of them only the usual dues, not the services. In addition, he granted them the right to fish in certain waters, and to hunt and to pasture on certain pieces of land.[10]

The rebels from Tring contented themselves with gaining exemption, on 16 June, from all toll within the liberty of St. Albans.[11]

But of all these charters, the most generous were those granted to Watford and Cashiobury, both drawn up in the same manner. The abbot acknowledged to the inhabitants of both these places an absolute right to hunt fowl on all the surrounding land, including the lord's land, he excused them from attending the monastery court, exempted them from a special tax called ale-penny, from rights of passage and from toll, and from compulsory work for the maintenance of bridges and roads, and finally allowed them to set up hand mills in their homes.[12] This charter was conceded only on 18 June — tit-bits for late-comers!

So, within a period of five days, from Sunday 16 June to Thursday 20 June, the abbey chancellery issued a series of letters granting freedoms and privileges to the peasants of the county who had flocked in at the news of the rising. There were thus two revolts in St. Albans: one by the townspeople, the other in pursuit of parallel interests by the other tenants of the monastery. These revolts, which were going on simultaneously, were different in their intensity but were equally successful in their outcome.

References, Chapter 2

1. *Hist. Anglic.*, I, 471; *Gesta*, III, 303.
2. *Hist. Anglic.*, I, 471-472; *Gesta*, III, 304.
3. ". . . Edmundus Cook, de Berk Hampstede, cum aliis de dicta villa, voluntarie venerunt ad villam de Sancto Albano die sabbati proximo post festum Corporis Christi . . ., et equitaverunt usque domum Roberti atte Chambre, et permanserunt ibidem super equos suos quousque illa domus coram cis prosternaretur, et dicunt quod (non) nesciunt nomina illorum de Berkhampstede, set erat (*sic*) quasi numero quadraginta. (*Coram rege, Mich. 5 Ric. II, m. 28*). — *Hist. Anglic.*, II, App. B, 394; *Gesta*, III, 328.
4. *Hist. Anglic.*, I, 481; *Gesta*, III, 317.
5. List of the towns which obtained charters from the abbot of St. Albans, in *Gesta*, III, 330.
6. *Hist. Anglic.*, II, App. B, 395; *Gesta*, III, 329-330. — *Rotuli Parliam.*, III, 129a, no. 10. — Cf. *Coram rege, Mich. 5 Ric. II, m. 31 dorso.*
7. *Gesta*, III, 330-331, with abstract; *Hist. Anglic.*, I, 483-484.
8. *Hist. Anglic.*, II, App. B, 394-395; *Gesta*, III, 328-329.
9. *Hist. Anglic.*, II, App. B, 394; *Gesta*, III, 324-328. The charter of Thomas de la Mare appears in *Gesta*, III, 324.
10. The author of *Gesta* (III, 325-327) copied two different versions of this charter.
11. Text of the charter: *Ibid.*, p. 327.
12. Text of the charter: *Ibid.*, p. 325.

CHAPTER 3. THE REVOLT IN THE REST OF THE COUNTY

Was St. Albans abbey the only place in Hertfordshire to be subject to assault during the revolt, and can the rising in Hertfordshire be represented simply as a struggle between Thomas de la Mare and his restless tenants? Were there not other rebels in the county besides the subjects of the abbey, other centres of unrest than the town of St. Albans?

It seems that the area to the north east, lying approximately between Baldock, Royston and Bishops Stortford, continued to enjoy relative peace even at the height of the storm: the revolt scarcely affected that area. It is true that there is evidence in the Parliamentary Rolls which seems to belie this assertion, since of the four rebels of Hertfordshire who were eventually to be excluded from the general amnesty one, William Bilche, was of Aldbury which is nine miles north east of Hertford, and another, John Coltman, was from the nearby village of Clavering.[1] But Clavering is situated not in Hertfordshire but in Essex: though close enough to north Hertfordshire, to explain the simple geographical error of the compilers of *Rotuli Parliamentorum*.[*] Apart from the case of William Bilche, neither the chronicles nor the diplomatic sources give any indication that the rising had spread into this north eastern area. The legal documents, abundant enough for the county of Hertfordshire, say nothing to support such a suggestion: certainly there was no centre of unrest in the region.

On the other hand, many incidents occurred in the southern part of the county. At Cheshunt, some miles south of Hertford, William Fyppe, on 14 June, forced entry into a house and carried off its contents:[2] on 15 June at Waltham Cross, even farther to the south, Walter Parshemener wounded William Patrik and another rebel finished him off.[3] Many supporters of the rising from Barnet and Watford were active in other parts of the county. One of them, Thomas Longe, arrived on 15 June at Digswell and forced his way into the house of John Lodewyk, a justice of the peace, and walked off with all his judicial papers and records. The next day he did the same at the house of another justice, John Kymperle.[4]

But it was along the western border of the county that the centres of revolt were most numerous and active. The rebels were strongest at Cashiobury, Langley, Hemel Hempstead and Berkhamsted. Some of them hastened on 15 June to St. Albans; others took action on their own account in their own neighbourhoods. William Wytton, for example, went into action with a group of others on 16 June. He went to Ashridge and burned the documents and the books of the priest there; then, at Kings Langley, he robbed a certain John Marlere of a tenure book which was in his possession.[5] Similarly, a little farther to the north another rebel, Percival Simeon, on 23 June, took by force from a widow, Agnes Holwell, property which she had inherited from her husband.[6] In the same region on 17 June a certain Richard Horsman put himself at the head of a band of rebels, made a standard consisting of the cross of St. George, and had it carried in front of him in various parts of the county where he issued a series of inflamatory proclamations. At Tring he

---

[*] Réville himself, however, seems to have confused Aldbury in west Hertfordshire with Albury in the east of the county. Thus, neither of these apparent exceptions really controverts his general conclusion that the north east of the county was untouched by the revolt.

105

burned the books, title deeds and other records of a manor belonging to the Archbishop of Canterbury.[7]

But in this western area it was at Redbourn and at Dunstable that the rising was most serious. The rebels of Redbourn had arrived at the abbey of St. Albans on the Saturday and joined in the excesses committed by the men of St. Albans. Having learned from that experience, they returned home and issued a proclamation — even though it was by then already getting dark — ordering all the inhabitants without exception, whether they were already in bed or still up, to meet together in a place which they appointed. Just as the rebels of St. Albans had converged on the abbey, they planned to attack the priory of Redbourn. They blamed the monks for having seized by force a meadow which belonged to the community in common. They proposed therefore to hurry to that meadow and break down the bank which surrounded it. No sooner said than done: when everyone had assembled at the rendezvous they all went off to carry out this plan, and in no time at all the bank was broken down and flattened, and several trees which had been planted upon it they cut down and carried off.[8]

The disturbance continued in the neighbourhood during the days which followed. Near to Redbourn is the village of Puttenham*, where the priest joined with others on Tuesday, 18 June, with the intention of killing a certain William Brag, servant of Edmund de Stonore. When they were unable to find him they burned the deeds and manorial rolls of his master. They found William Brag some days later in a nearby village, and beat him to death with staves.[9]

At Dunstable, as at Redbourn, there was a priory, so it is not surprising that "the devil gave full rein there to his wickedness", as the chronicler put it. A number of traders from Dunstable had gone to the market at St. Albans on the Saturday when all the violence was directed against the abbey, setting an unhappy precedent for the rest of the county. These traders were the sort of people who have only to see something and they must copy it. They returned to Dunstable and arrived at the priory just before the hour of vespers. Their leader, Thomas Hobbes, who was the chief rebel of the town, accosted the prior, Thomas Marchal, and greeted him in the name of the king, whereupon the prior lowered his hood, inclined his head politely, and asked what Richard II wanted of him. "He summonses and orders you", replied Thomas Hobbes in a threatening manner, "to draw up a charter for the townspeople of Dunstable, like the one they had in the time of King Henry I".

The prior started to refuse but thought better of it, remembering all that had befallen London and St. Albans. He gave way, and the document was drafted, sealed, and handed over to the rebels. By this act the inhabitants of Dunstable acknowledged for all time that the prior was their rightful lord, but they obtained certain privileges: in particular, butchers and fishmongers from the surrounding countryside were forbidden to sell their meat and fish within the town.[10] This clause deserves notice, since it illustrates how the revolt had various and conflicting effects in different counties. At Mile End the insurgents of Essex had obliged the king to authorise complete liberty to trade in the towns as in the countryside, and as a result of that confrontation Richard II had decreed, by letters patent, that in future every person should have the right to buy and sell his merchandise anywhere,

* Puttenham is in fact 3 miles to the north-west of Tring, about 12 miles west of Redbourn.

regardless of any other privileges. At Dunstable the townspeople had wrung from the prior contrary concessions. Yet they shared the same motivation: the risings in London and in Hertfordshire had taken place within a matter of hours, and all the rebels regarded one another as allies. The revolt, which resulted from a great variety of grievances, represented a pooling of often contradictory interests in a common cause.

References, Chapter 3

1. *Rotuli Parliam.*, III, 111b.
2. *Coram rege, Trin. 5 Ric. II, m. 21.*
3. *Ibid., Easter 5 Ric. II, m. 23; Mich. 5 Ric. II, m. 43 dorso.*
4. ". . . Thomas Longe, de Watford, fuit voluntarie cum comitiva iniqua que surrexit adversus dominum regem . . . circa festum Corporis Christi, et . . . nunc [venit] ad domum Johannis Lodewyk, justiciarii domini regis ad pacem in comitatu Hertfordie conservandum assignati, apud Dikeswell, et ibidem clausa et domos ipsius Johannis Lodewyk ibidem proditorie et felonice fregit, et recordum, processus, et indictamenta dicti domini regis in custodia ipsius Johannis ibidem existencia cepit et asportavit, die sabati proximo post festum Corporis Christi . . . Et . . . idem Thomas Longe, die dominica proxima post predictum festum Corporis Christi . . . venit proditorie ad domum Johannis Kymperle in villa predicta, et fecit eidem Johanni deliberari sibi recordum et processus ac alios libros domini regis, ac commissionem pacis domini regis per quam idem Johannes et alii ad pacem predictam conservandam assignati fuerant de comitatu; iidem (*sic*) Thomas recordum, processus, libros ac commissionem predictam extra custodiam dicti Johannis felonice et proditorie asportavit, et eos arseri (*sic*) voluisset ex auctoritate sua propria, ac eciam plures libros ejusdem domini regis ad domum Johannis Lodewyk quesivit". (*Coram rege, Trin. 5 Ric. II, m. 33*).
5. "Willelmus Wytton primus, simul cum aliis proditoribus qui surrexerunt contra etc. et contra ligeanciam suam, surrexerunt apud Berkhampstede ut inimici regis, die dominica proxima post festum Corporis Christi, anno etc., at abinde usque Assherugg iverunt, et ibidem libros, munimenta rectoris de Assherugge felonice et proditorie combusserunt, et abinde usque Kyngeslangele iverunt manu forti, et contra ligeanciam suam ibidem Johannem Marlere de libero tenemento suo in eadem villa [dissaisiverunt]." (*Coram rege, Mich. 5 Ric, II, m. 34*). — Cf. *Annales de Dunstaplia*, p. 417, for mention of the revolt at Ashridge.
6. ". . . Persevallus Symyon simul cum aliis malefactoribus, die dominica proxima ante festum Nativitatis sancti Johannis Baptiste . . ., proditorie, armata potencia et modo guerrino, et per minas societatum contra legem insurgencium, disseisivit Agnetem Holwelle de tenemento quondam Michaelis Holwell, viri ipsius Agnetis, cum pertinenciis suis, in Hatfield Episcopi". (*Coram rege, Trin. 5 Ric. II, m. 24 dorso*). Cf. *Rot. Litt. claus, 5 Ric. II, m. 40*, which makes it clear that Percival Simeon was a landowner.
7. ". . . Fecit quoddam vexillum de armis sancti Georgii, et ivit cum predicto vexillo in diversis partibus comitatus Hertfordie, et fecit quasdam proclamaciones ut homines de comitatu predicto surgerent . . ., ac eciam libros, munimenta et rotulos archiepiscopi Cantuariensis de Trenge, apud Trenge, prodiciose et felonice arcit". (*Coram rege, Mich. 6 Ric. II, m. 27*).
8. *Hist. Anglic.*, II, App. B, 395; *Gesta*, III, 329. — [For a reference to the arrest of an inhabitant of Redbourn "pro suspecione insurreccionis proditorie versus dominum regem", see *Coram rege, Mich. 5 Ric. II, m. 27 dorso*].
9. "Rex dilectis et fidelibus suis Johanni de Aylesbury, Thomas Sakevyll, Thome atte Lude et Rogero Colyn, salutem. Ad vestram satis sufficienter pervenit noticiam qualiter Hugo the personespriest of Puttenham, Willelmus Ffordham, Walterus Ffreman, Ricardus Merston, Ricardus Baldok, Thomas Baldok et Ricardus Ffordham, ac nonulli alii malefactores . . . cartas, literas, rentallia et alia munimienta (*sic*) dilecti nobis Edmundi de Stonore et aliorum ligeorum nostrorum proditorie et felonice combusserunt . . .; apud Cublecote accesserunt et Willelmum Brag, servientem ipsius Edmundi, ibidem nequiter interfecerunt, et alia dampna quamplurima ibidem perpetrarunt, et eidem Edmundo ac aliis ligeis nostris, si quicquam versus eos ex hac causa prosequi presumpserint, interficiendi ac domos suas comburendi manifeste sunt comminati". (*Pat. 5 Ric. II, part 1, m. 1 dorso*). Inquest on the misdeeds of "Hugh the 'personespriest' de Putenham" and his accomplices: *Coram rege, Mich. 6 Ric. II, m. 5*.
10. *Annales de Dunstaplia*, p. 417-418.

CHAPTER 4. CHARACTERISTICS OF THE REVOLT IN HERTFORDSHIRE

To sum up: the conflagration spread, little by little, till it covered the greater part of Hertfordshire. The first sparks were struck at Barnet, then at St. Albans where they kindled a flame which spread to the south and west of the county, from Cheshunt to Tring and from Walden* to Rickmansworth. Only the area in the north east remained free of any significant ravages.

The disturbance lasted for only twelve days: it broke out on 13 June, assumed serious proportions at St. Albans from the 14th to the 16th, and continued there till Thursday the 20th, already dwindling but not entirely spent. In the west, where it began some hours later, it also persisted for some days longer.[1] So much is revealed about the history of the rising of 1381 in Hertfordshire by the evidence contained in diplomatic and narrative sources. But to probe no farther would be to neglect the most important part of this study. This evidence has told us only what the rebels did. We must reach out beyond that, to the people, and even if possible to their motives. That is the end and the justification of history.

Let us therefore try to determine in what state of mind the people of Hertfordshire rebelled, what was their purpose, and how they expected to achieve it.

It was certainly not political ideals which incited them to rebellion, like their brothers and allies of Kent and London. We find in their statements no reference to the notorious poll-tax of 1381, which elsewhere had such an important bearing on the outbreak of the rising. They do not lay the blame on John of Gaunt and, although they were at London on Friday, 14 June, they probably did not associate themselves with the murderers of the chancellor and the treasurer. The rebellion in Kent produced Jack Straw, who had a vision of a reallocation of authority on new lines; the rebellion in Hertfordshire produced only William Grindecob, who was capable of seeking an alliance with the idealists of London, but who did not dream of supporting their grand design because his horizon was limited and his ambitions were purely local ones.

Thus, the rising here had nothing to do with politics. Nor had it in the least a religious character, and that is a conclusion of some interest, since some people have connected the revolt of 1381 with the influence of the ideas of Wycliffe. Without entering into a general discussion on that point, it is permissible to affirm that the conduct of the rebels in Hertfordshire does not support such a view: there were no Lollards among them, or the chronicler of St. Albans, who abhorred that heresy, would not have failed to direct this additional accusation towards them, and indeed to make it the most serious of their crimes.

The revolt in this county, furthermore, was not a great orgy of pillaging, as in some parts of Norfolk. There were undoubtedly some thefts committed under cover of the troubles, at Cheshunt and Kings Langley for example, but such cases were rare. At St. Albans, where there was a general rising, we find only one example: a certain Richard Lokyere forced the vicar of St. Peter's church to give him ten shillings, threatening if he refused to destroy his house.[2] These are the only exceptions which one can cite. Rebellions always attract a fringe of people, not committed to the cause, who only stir up trouble for their own ends,

* This is possibly a mistake for Waltham, in the east of the county.

and it is remarkable that in Hertfordshire there was not more of that sort of thing. The chroniclers aver that the insurgents of Kent had established a stern discipline in their ranks, and that theft was severely punished. We don't know whether similar steps were taken in Hertfordshire, but the result was the same, and it is to the credit of the rebels.

So the rebels of Hertfordshire were neither Lollards, nor political opportunists as in Kent, nor plunderers like the insurgents of Norfolk. Their rebellion had above all a social objective: it was a rising of tenants against their feudal lords. They sought only to enjoy certain rights: to pasture their cattle, to hunt, to fish, to grind corn. The people of St. Albans, of Redbourn, of Dunstable and elsewhere were determined to seize some part of their rights. This was so clearly their goal that the rebels fixed upon it right at the beginning of the revolt, pursued it steadily, attained it, and did not attempt to go beyond it. Drunk with success, they could have tried to shake off the protection of their lord, renouncing their contract of allegiance. They did nothing of the kind. At St. Albans, it is true, they obtained assurances that the abbot would not interfere in the government of the town; but they did not repudiate his overlordship, and in the charter which they dictated to the clerks of Thomas de la Mare they described themselves as the abbot's townspeople: "Abbas . . . burgensibus suis, salutem". At Dunstable they went one better, and in the undertaking which they extracted from the prior they specified that they recognised him as their rightful lord. The chronicler recorded this with some surprise: "Et nota", said he, "quod in charta illa, quam a nobis ita pertinaciter exigebant, continetur quod fidelitatem domino priori facere debent".[3] This clearness of conception and this moderation in the moment of success deserve to be recalled, for both are rare in times of revolution.

The rising of the peasants of Hertfordshire was also of a social character when seen from another point of view: a large number of villein-tenants demanded that the royal charter of liberties, granted after the confrontation at Mile End, should be applied to themselves, and that the abbot of St. Albans should ratify it for their use. However, the status of villeins was not a dominant issue in this county: it occupied no place in the claims of the townspeople; it was a graft upon the main trunk of the revolt rather than one of its roots. It sprang up because circumstances were favourable but it was not part of the motivation of the revolt.[4]

Thus, the rising in Hertfordshire was of a social nature, but in the most positive and practical sense of the word. Its object was to improve the conditions under which the tenants were dependent on their lord, whether he was the abbot of St. Albans, the prior of Redbourn or the prior of Dunstable.

What steps did the rebels take to achieve this objective? They acted with very considerable energy. On the first day of the revolt the inhabitants of St. Albans covered more than 40 miles, and on their return from London, without taking an hour's rest, they made their first attack on the abbey before it had time to put itself into a state of defence. This energy did not stop short of violence, as the breaking down of fences and the devastation of warrens bear witness. If that violence showed limited intelligence, at least it was seldom bloody, and that is a very remarkable thing when one recalls how frequently there was bloodshed elsewhere, and especially when one thinks about the customs of the times, when acts of violence occurred daily, when innumerable bands roamed the country, occupying manors, mutilating, killing, exacting ransoms from people, in such great force that the officers responsible for public protection dared not to try to enforce the law, when everyone went armed, with his hand on his sword.[5] Drastic and violent though they were, it seems that the rebels of Hertfordshire hesitated to shed blood.

They conducted their campaign, moreover, with considerable skill. They left St. Albans in the middle of the night, deceiving Thomas de la Mare as to their intentions, remained in London only long enough to assure themselves of help, and succeeded within a few hours in setting up two alliances — even two opposing alliances — one with Wat Tyler and one with the king, thus making certain, or believing that they were making certain, of being supported whatever might be the outcome. On their return the abbot, who had been fooled by these cunning peasants, had no choice but to submit to their demands.

They established their claim, not on the basis of natural right or on abstract reasoning, but on historic traditions, demanding a return to the good old times of Henry I. These were much the same sentiments as those which in previous revolts had sought a return to the conditions of King Offa, and which in 1377 demanded of parliament a copy of Domesday Book in order to base their claims on that venerable text.[6]

But the rights of their antagonists, the monks, were founded on records no less worthy of respect, on ancient charters, on title deeds whose authenticity no-one, not even the rebels, could deny. That obvious consideration did not deter them for an instant: with a resolution which testified to their naive simplicity, they burned them, convinced that once these documents had been destroyed the provisions which they contained were also annulled. Then they themselves drafted new charters of privileges, without suspecting that their lords, when restored to power, would be able to suppress these useless writings just as they themselves had destroyed the others. They were animated by an awed respect for parchment, but only when it suited their ends: a childish conception, but one which in various degrees, and in a form sometimes more sophisticated, sometimes less, is in evidence at all times. Everywhere revolutionaries destroy things and then in their place erect new structures in the belief that they will survive the passage of time, whereas they too are only houses of cards.

The rebel of Hertfordshire was, in short, a tenant as represented in the Vision of Piers Ploughman — "working and restless, as the world requires, toiling with great effort, labouring hard". Life in the open air in a hard climate, accustomed to heavy physical labour and hard knocks, had given him strong muscles and a resilient character. He was capable of dogged resolve and tireless action. His senses were slow, his perceptions imprecise; he had no personal views on politics or religion; he had no time for dreaming and no idea of reforming society; his notions were entirely positive and practical, and since his horizon was narrow they all concerned himself and his own property. He knew very clearly what he lacked, was quick to seize the chance of securing it, and cunning enough to be successful. He was sufficiently master of himself not to lose sight for an instant of the objective he was pursuing, and to stop when it had been achieved. He was sufficiently suspicious not to believe the assurances of others and to demand written documents, but naive enough to believe that his own achievements would last for ever, because he was incapable of taking the long-term view. He was a man of strong feelings beneath a cold exterior, not afraid to lay waste his lord's property, to demolish his houses, to break down his fences; but his moral sense was well developed, and he was too honest to rob or to kill. To sum up, he was physically strong, of limited but practical intelligence, and basically honest at heart: in fact, a typical peasant of the north.

References, Chapter 4
1. See *Assize Rolls*, N. 2, 29, 4, m. 47 and 47 dorso. — *Coram rege, Trin. 5 Ric. II, m. 24 dorso.*
2. *Coram rege, Trin. 5 Ric. II, m. 33.*
3. *Annales de Dunstaplia*, p. 418.
4. [Because of the scarcity of diplomatic documents regarding the revolt in Hertfordshire, André Réville was unable to give details of the social origins of the rebels. It is clear, however, that they included people from all ranks of society, not just the poorest. A letter patent of 1386 gives some information about John Wilkyn, one of the rebels who were first to experience the king's vengeance. He possessed a dwelling-house, three outhouses, 164 acres of arable land (*Patent 9 Ric. II, part. 2, m. 24*). Thomas Skot, who was tried at St. Albans on 18 July 1381, "pro felonia et prodicionibus quas fecit", possessed a house and garden, 50 acres of arable land, 4 acres of meadow, 8 acres of pasture and 2 acres of woodland. He had bought the whole of this property in 1373. (*Claus. 6 Ric. II, part 1, m. 17*). We have seen elsewhere that William Grindecob also possessed some property.]
5. To convince ourselves that this picture is by no means exaggerated, we need do no more than look through the Patent Rolls of 1380 and the early part of 1381. [For example, on 25 June 1380, a writ from Richard II to the sheriff of Worcester ordering him to seize a band of robbers (*Patent 4 Ric. II, part. 1, m. 43 dorso*); on the following 12 July, a writ of 'Oyer and Terminer' concerning a criminal gang "in magno numero, sacramento confederati et modo guerrino arraiati" in Devonshire. (*Ibid., m. 36 dorso*). Identical writs concerned organised bands in various other counties. These ruffians would descend upon houses, farms and monasteries, assaulting the occupants and carrying off cattle and movables. (*Ibid., m. 34 dorso, 33d, 26d, 23d, 18d, 15d, 6d, 4d, 2d; part. 2, m. 26d, 19d, 3d, 1d. — Patent 5 Ric. II, part. 1, m. 11d, 7d; part. 2, m. 35d, 27d, 23d.*) See also *Rotul. Parliam., III, 71 no. 3, 81 et seq., 96 no. xxiv, 102 no. 24. — Statutes of the Realm, I, 6-11, 27.* — Cf. Jusserand, *English wayfaring life*, chap. III: Security of the roads, and by the same author *Le Théâtre en Angleterre*, p. 17-18. — It is characteristic of the violence of the times that women were often to be found in the bands of robbers and murderers referred to above, and even churchmen did not shrink from getting mixed up with them. A writ of 1384 referred to an armed band which included an abbot, two vicars and a clerk in holy order. (See *Pat. 8 Ric. II, part. 1, m. 36d.*)]
6. Stubbs, *Constitutional history*, 4th ed., II, 477, note 1.

CHAPTER 5. SUBMISSION OF THE REBELS

As we have noted, the rebels in Hertfordshire stopped of their own accord once their goal was achieved. They dispersed, disarmed, returned to their houses and resumed their daily work. It was therefore unnecessary to oppose them by force: all that was needed was to get them to give up, of their own accord or by force, the charters of liberties which they had extorted from their lords. That done, their revolt would be reduced to no more than a memory. In Suffolk and Norfolk, on the other hand, the rebels remained in arms and organised into resistence groups, some of which laid waste the fields, others held the city of Norwich, and all together exercised effective control over the countryside. In Hertfordshire it was necessary only to punish the rebellion; in the two other counties it was first necessary to bring it to an end . . .

After the damage and violence to which the abbey of St. Albans had been subjected, the abbot had addressed to the king a long letter in the French language — if one can so describe his jargon — in which he made a series of charges against the rebels, listed their crimes and demanded justice.[1] It is clear that he had no faith in his own supporters and looked for salvation to Richard II and his ministers. By this time peace had been restored in London, and Kent had been quietened as a result of the action of the nobility who at last had taken the initiative in resisting the rebels.[2] Essex however was still in turmoil, and Richard went there in person, in the last days of June, at the head of his levies. From Essex he sent to St. Albans a commissioner, Sir Walter atte Lee, charged with re-establishing peace between the villeins and the monastery — which meant, in other words, restoring to the abbey the concessions which the rebels had extorted from it.

When the rebels of St. Albans learned that Walter atte Lee was approaching with fifty mounted men and a large number of archers (though these had been raised from the countryside, and were of doubtful reliability) many were fearful and would have been inclined to flee if William Grindecob had not strongly opposed such a course "with his villainous stubbornness". He reassured them, reminded them that all the neighbouring villages were on their side, and proposed to them, not without guile, that they should go on horseback to meet the royal commissioner and welcome him with goodwill if he came with peaceful proposals, but remain free to drive him off if he came as an enemy.

The commissioner arrived on the morning of 28 June, affecting the most conciliatory intentions, and the rebels escorted him into town. This exchange of pleasantries was no more than a lure, but the deception was maintained in the days that followed; and the contrast between the apparent and real sentiments on both sides was most marked during the negotiations on which they embarked. Extreme courtesy was combined with extreme tenacity, the one side seeking to regain possession of stolen charters, the other intending to hold on to them, and everyone protesting their peaceful intentions and goodwill.

On the day of his arrival, Sir Walter made a public proclamation, calling upon the villeins to meet together in three hours time at the edge of a wood which specified. Everyone came to the rendezvous. If the account of the chronicler is correct — and everything indicates that he was well-informed — Walter atte Lee tried at one and the same time to flatter them, to over-awe them, and to present himself in a favourable light.

He called them 'lords' and 'friends' ('*domini et amici*'), then he painted for them a dreadful picture of the ravages of the royal army which was bringing to Essex "a heavy and severe justice", putting those who disturbed the peace back beneath a yoke heavier than before, and commandeering on its passage all the fruit and corn for five miles around. If they were to avoid the same miseries it would be thanks to him, who had been sent in advance of the king himself to pacify the countryside. He advised them, as a friend, to give satisfaction to the abbot, and he immediately appointed twelve villeins and charged them to come on the following day, in accordance with the custom of English law, to accuse under oath all those whom they knew to be at fault.

On the following day these jurymen declared that they would not or could not accuse anyone, seeing that they were all good and faithful subjects of the king, and that they did not know any among themselves who were culpable. Sir Walter did not press the point, and advised them only to hand over to the abbot the charters which they had wrested from him, adding that they would earn his commendation by this action. Always appearing well disposed, they replied that they would return those documents within three hours; but three hours later they came back without the charters, saying by way of excuse that they did not know exactly who was holding them and that besides they feared the fury of the people.

The royal commissioner then called on them to assemble outside the town for a second time. The crowd was more numerous even than before, having been augmented by a good number of rebels brought together from the surrounding countryside, notably from Barnet and Berkhamsted. Sir Walter contented himself with producing yet more fine words and advising the restitution of the charters. When it was clear that he was not going to get them, he decided on bold action. Calling together in secret the town bailiffs, he ordered them on the morrow to arrest and convey to Hertford the three principal leaders, Grindecob, Cadingdone and John Barbour, and he directed certain knights in the service of the abbot — Richard Perers, John Chival, Thomas Eydon, and William Eccleshale — to escort the convoy. Meanwhile he himself left immediately with his own party for Hertford — a prudent if not very courageous action. The following day the arrest was made, thanks to the presence of the knights, and the three accused were led away to confront their adversary, who had become their judge.

At the news of this stroke, tumult broke out in the town. The rebels, after much to-ing and fro-ing, gathered together and swore vengeance, then ran amok in the fields and woods and threatened to set fire to the abbey or to beseige it, causing the terrified inmates to send hastily to the knights in Hertford and beg them to come to their aid. They returned to St. Albans, and Walter atte Lee, persuaded perhaps by the general disquiet, released Grindecob on bail for the very considerable sum of three hundred pounds, making it clear to his sureties that he would be brought back to prison on the following Saturday if a peaceful settlement was not concluded in the meantime.

There was a lot of sense in Sir Walter's reasoning: that Grindecob, who could see death not far off, having to choose between the gibbet and the return of the charters, would think only of escaping punishment and use his influence on his rebellious companions to persuade them to give away. He deceived himself. Grindecob, with a stubborness which

113

was not without nobility, put the cause of his people above his own interest, and made use of his last hours of freedom to stiffen their resistence. "Act today", was his message, "as you would if I had been executed yesterday". This is attested by Walsingham, who was well placed to be accurately informed on the matter, and moreover had no interest in extolling the heroism of one of the enemies of the abbey. There is therefore no reason to doubt his testimony, and this new Regulus would have been an entirely authentic successor to the original, but for the fact that his brother went straightaway to the king at Chelmsford in order to intercede in his favour.

The rebels remained intractable, and on Saturday, 6 July, in accordance with his undertaking, William Grindecob returned to prison where he was to remain this time until the day of his judgement.

The mission of Sir Walter atte Lee had reached complete stalemate, and the people were savouring their triumph when they learned that the king, determined to bring them to their senses, had sent to St. Albans the Earl of Warwick and Sir Thomas Percy, with a thousand armed men. At this news, which they got to know about on Friday, 5 July, through Grindecob's brother, their elation turned, it seems, to dread, and from the next day, when they once again lost their leader and their main support, their morale was very low and they humbled themselves before the abbot. They went to the monastery towards the hour of compline, taking back their charters of liberties and a certain book which contained the ancient agreements between the monks and the villeins and which they had stolen on the first day of the rising. Besides this they offered a fine of two hundred pounds. But Thomas de la Mare, who was also awaiting the arrival of the avenging royal troops, would not receive them. He sent them a monk, William Kyllingworth, who invited them to come again the next day, but who retained in his own care the precious volume of agreements.

On the following day they learned that the Earl of Warwick, recalled to his own lordship by disturbances which had suddenly broken out there, would not after all be coming to St. Albans; he had merely sent to the abbot a certain number of knights for his defence. This news reassured the rebels, who once more went from one extreme to the other in a rather childish vacillation. They cheered themselves up, made light of their fears, regained their courage and, with their morale restored, refused to hand over the charters, claiming it is true that their companions from Watford and Barnet were preventing them from doing so.

Their relief was short-lived, for they soon learned that the king himself, having completed his sweep through Essex, was coming in person to put an end to their outrages. Strangely enough, this news was equally disturbing to the rebels and to their victims, on the one hand because with Richard II came punishment; on the other because the king and his followers were allies and guests as burdensome as they were useful. The abbot beseeched the seneschal of London, and other members of the privy council, to prevent by any means the arrival of the sovereign, but they replied that the king would be at the monastery within two days. As for the rebels, they were stripped immediately, as if by magic, of their composure. No longer daring to present themselves before the abbey, they sent there as spokesman a knight to whom they paid a very large sum to plead in their favour. Thomas de la Mare consented to forgive them and drew up the following agreement with his enemies:

1. They would bring back, on the same day that the king arrived, the stone slabs which they had pulled up from the floor of the parlour, and they would rebuild with their own hands a house belonging to the abbey which they had destroyed.
2. They would pay to the monks two hundred pounds for damages and interest before 25 September next.
3. The abbot would make no complaint against them before the king, and if the king should pursue them he would make every effort to secure their pardon.[3]

They executed this document, promised to observe its provisions, repaired the damage they had done to the parlour of the monastery, and gave up their charters — not, however, without keeping several copies, to the great annoyance of the abbot who later was to complain of it in parliament.[4]

Everything was therefore under control when the king entered St. Albans on Friday, 12 July. All the inhabitants, rebels and monks, went together to receive him in great pomp and with all the marks of the most profound respect. But the insurgents could not have been under the least illusion as to the purpose of his visit to the abbey, and the task which he intended to carry out. He was indeed escorted by a very great number of archers, and in his entourage there was to be found a lawyer whom the rebels were going to get to know to their cost — Sir Robert Tresilian, Chief Justice of England.[5]

However, with the tenacity of country folk they did not entirely abandon the hope of preserving some of their new liberties, and they did not give up the struggle. They pronounced the abbot a hypocrite, guilty of deceiving visitors by his holy appearance, of having taken away from the people of St. Albans their rights and their ancient liberties, and of being a tyrant and oppressing his tenants. Rumours to this effect, which the townsmen — the wives, too, more cleverly than the husbands — spread among the king's subjects, were so numerous and so persistent that recourse was had to proclamation: the men would be hanged who spread such slanders about the monastery, and the women burned.[6]

For the rest, it was like an encounter between an earthenware pot and a pot of iron. Richard lodged at the abbey. He had installed his court of chancery in the principal room, and the abbot presided.[7] As from 15 July, a royal decree annulled in his favour all the concessions extorted by the rebels: the king made it clear to John Lodewyk, John West-Wycombe, John Kentyng, Richard Peres and several others, that the tenants of the monastery must render to their lords the same services and pay the same dues as before; he ordered them to make a general proclamation and to arrest any recalcitrants. This was an amplification, with special reference to the abbey, of the general decree issued on 30 June.[8]

The prior of Dunstable also took advantage of the presence of the king at St. Albans for the purpose of re-establishing all his rights. As the townspeople refused to restore to him the charter which they had extorted from him, he appealed to Richard, who called before him representatives of the inhabitants and annulled the privileges which they had obtained unlawfully.[9]

Then on 20 July the king received the oath of fealty of all the inhabitants of Hertfordshire between 15 and 60 years of age, called together for this purpose in the courtyard of the abbey. They undertook to be faithful in the future, to die rather than obey at any time those who would stir up troubles, and to restrain any who might be tempted to renew the disorders. Then they withdrew.

When peace had been finally re-established in the town and its environs, Richard, having done what he set out to do in St. Albans, resumed his progress to restore order, stopping next at Berkhamsted. Little is known about the role which he played in that locality, but everything suggests that his objective there was the same as at the abbey, namely to pacify the countryside and restore to the lords their ancient privileges. It was not long before he left that town also for his estate of East-Hampstead, where he found in hunting a relaxation from fatigue and a diversion from his fears. [10]

References, Chapter 5

   1. *Gesta*, III, 289-296.
   2. *Patent 4 Ric. II, part. 3, m. 4; 5 Ric. II, part. 1, m. 33.*
   3. This is taken from the very detailed account by Walsingham, *Hist. Anglic.*, II, 22-31, reproduced in *Gesta*, III, 334-346.
   4. *Hist. Anglic.*, II, 31; *Gesta*, III, 347. — *Rot. Parliam., III, 129 a, no. 10.*
   5. *Chron. Angl.*, 320: *Hist. Anglic.*, II, 31; *Gesta abbatum*, III, 347. — John Malverne, in *Polychronicon*, IX, 7.
   6. *Hist. Anglic.*, II, 37-38; *Gesta abbatum*, III, 351-352.
   7. *Hist. Anglic.*, II, 38; *Gesta abbatum*, III, 352.
   8. Letters published in *Chron. Angliae*, 324-325; *Hist. Anglic.*, II, 38-39; *Gesta*, III, 353.
   9. *Annales de Dunstaplia*, p. 418-419.
  10. *Chron. Angl.*, 325; *Hist. Anglic.*, II, 39; *Gesta*, III, 354.

CHAPTER 6. JUDICIAL ACTION

So in Hertfordshire, as in Suffolk and Norfolk, after only a few days the rebellion was suppressed and its effects annulled. The insurrection was quite over; expiation was about to begin. It was supervised at St. Albans by the Chief Justice in person, the King's Treasurer Sir Robert Tresilian. The chronicler of St. Albans wrote most highly of him: "He was a knight, a judge of great skill, a man of simple courage and the cunning of a serpent".[1]

Unhappily he was at one and the same time both the judge and a party to the conflict which he had been given the job of settling. His profession in effect made him the enemy of the rebels, because he was one of those men of law whom above all others they had hounded with their hatred and their violence, and his predecessor Sir John de Cavendish had fallen beneath their blows. The impartiality of Sir Robert was therefore open to doubt, though the danger which might result from this was minimised in a country where no judge, however powerful, could condemn an innocent man unless he was accused by twelve sworn eye-witnesses and declared guilty by twelve more. Sometimes, moreover, the accused party, finding his cause lost, might give up at this last trial and throw himself on the king's mercy; and one can also find, in the process that followed the revolt, one or two examples of trial by combat. But these were exceptional cases, always voluntarily undertaken, never imposed, and one can say that trial by inquest was almost universal.

From Saturday, 13 July, the day after his arrival, in the presence of the king, Tresilian had established his tribunal at St. Albans, in the Moothall.[2]* By strange coincidence, one of the first of the rebels that he had to judge was a stranger to Hertfordshire, the "foolish priest of Kent", John Ball, one of the leaders and instigators of the rising in the south. He had hidden himself for several days from the searches of the royal officers, but when discovered at Coventry was arrested and led before the king who was then at St. Albans, and proceedings were instituted against him by Tresilian. No-one doubted his culpability, and the sentence was a foregone conclusion. He had, besides, a very fierce and almost scornful expression. When accused of having fomented and instigated the revolt, he admitted everything with which he was charged; he acknowledged his authorship of the inflammatory letters which had circulated secretly at the time of the rising; he offered no defence, and "would not ask for the mercy of the king, whom he scorned".[3] His avowals earned for him a sentence of death, but he brought upon himself a multitude of punishments: he was condemned to be successively drawn on a hurdle, hanged, decapitated, disembowelled, and cut into quarters.[4] That was a great deal of punishment for a single body, but the gibbet, which took precedence, cancelled nearly all the rest. Anyway, he had been one of the leaders of the revolt, inspirer of more than one crime. The condemned man was accorded a delay before execution, which was regarded as a favour. His death was put back for two days on the intervention of William Courtenay, Bishop of London and future Archbishop of Canterbury. This prelate obtained for John Ball, who was a priest, time to collect himself and repent his sins, and it was only on Monday, 15 July, that he was

* This building, much altered, still exists at the corner of Dagnall Street and Market Place. It is at present occupied W. H. Smith and Son Ltd.

117

executed under the eyes of the king.[5]

At the same time, Tresilian had begun the trial of the rebels of St. Albans. Since Saturday he had brought together twelve witnesses and had obtained out of their own mouths, on oath, the names of the leaders of the revolt and details of their individual crimes. He had also ordered to be brought from Hertford, where they were still in prison, William Grindecob, William Cadingtone and John Barbour.[6]

If we can believe the chronicler, various inhabitants of the town bore witness against the abbey: they accused Thomas de la Mare and his monks of having fomented the rising, and made them go against their wills and join the London rioters, when they themselves had no thought of doing such a thing. Tresilian asked them only whether they believed, in all conscience, that the abbot had acted to betray the king, and not to prevent the coming of the rebels. He placed them on oath, and as he pressed them they acknowledged that Thomas de la Mare had not betrayed the king and had believed that he acted for the best. Having obtained this verification, Tresilian ordered them to tear up the deed of accusation which they had drawn up — which they did with some misgivings — and he chided them severely.[7]

Several days later, Tresilian suspended his judicial action, for what reason is not clear though in all probability because he moved on with the king. He returned some months later, and on 15 October he opened at St. Albans a second series of assizes. Since the king was no longer present, and the men at arms were no longer so blatantly menacing, the people of Hertfordshire showed an inclination from the outset to resist. When the Chief Justice, having brought together the same jurors who in July had indicated to him the instigators of the rebellion, asked them to renew their depositions, they replied that they did not know of any traitor, that they could accuse no-one, that their fellow citizens were obedient and faithful subjects and had always been so. Tresilian replied very simply that on the arrival of the king they had come forward to implore his mercy, but that they only obtained it by denouncing the instigators of the troubles. Should they now refuse, they would be the ones who would suffer the punishment of the guilty. Then he showed them the deeds of accusation drawn up in July, proving to them by this means that he was well-informed and that their silence would be of no use. Frightened, they gave in and denounced a good number of the rebels, from the town and the country round about. He brought together again two groups of witnesses who confirmed the former depositions, so that no-one was condemned at St. Albans without having been accused by 36 jurors.[8]

Retribution after the rising was not particularly rigorous: far from it, in Hertfordshire. Fifteen rebels only were hanged in the county, remarkably few after a popular rising. Naturally Grindecob, Cadingdone, and Barbour were among them. But other like Richard of Wallingford and Thomas Payntor who had taken a prominent part in the revolt, were only imprisoned.

From the neighbourhood of St. Albans there were imprisoned 80 persons in all. The majority of these were not long in obtaining their release, and from 20 October 1381 to 28 May 1382 one can find in the Chancery Roll in the Public Record Office no fewer than 24 letters of remission in favour of insurgents in Hertfordshire. Furthermore, the chroniclers of St. Albans and Dunstable both claim for their superiors the honour of having interceded repeatedly in favour of the prisoners.[9]

It seems that the counsellors of Richard II, with a moderation so much more praise-worthy because of its rarity in times of revolution, aimed not to make martyrs of the rebels but to frighten them by working on their imaginations. It was to this end no doubt that they forbade St. Albans to take down from the gibbet the convicted rebels who had suffered the final punishment, or to bury their remains. The corpses were to remain in the open air, exposed to the ravages of time and under the eyes of the populace, until the day when, by themselves, they should fall to dust — or, to use the harsh legal expression, so long as they endured (*quamdiu durare possent*').

Such a place was dreary, humiliating, repulsive, perhaps even worse,[10] and it is easy to understand that it seemed unbearable to the inhabitants. So in spite of the royal prohibition, they carried off their dead and buried them. Richard, "wondering at their audacity and not a little upset at the affront which they had offered to him", punished the culprits and ordered them to rehang the bodies. "We instruct you", he wrote on 3 August from East Hampstead to the bailiff of St. Albans, "touching your fealty and your allegience . . ., to fashion chains of iron to put back on the gibbets the above-mentioned corpses, wherever they may be, and to hang them by these iron chains".

These instructions were carried out. What remained of the bodies were painfully dis-interred and replaced on the gibbet.[12] Eventually the king softened a little and allowed them to receive the last rites, and we can still read in the Patent Rolls the following authorisation:

"Know that on the supplication of our dear Queen Anne, we have given authority to the bailiff and constable of St. Albans, and to all others, to bury the bones of the rebels who were punished by death after the revolt, without hindrance from anyone".[13]

But this order is dated only 3 September 1382. These unfortunate men had therefore been hanging from the gibbet for nearly fourteen months.

1. *Chron. Angl.*, 320; *Hist. Anglic.*, II, 31; *Gesta*, III, 347.

2. [Judgements commenced on 12 July, according to a letter patent dated 20 March 1386. This concerned land confiscated by Robert Basset, escheator for the county of Hertford, from John Wilkyn, who had been convicted of treason at St. Albans, 12 July 1381. *Patent 9 Ric. II, p. 2, m. 24.*]

3. *Vita Ricardi*, p. 33 — John Malverne, in *Polychronicon*, IX, 7.

4. *Chron. Angl.*, 320; *Hist. Anglic.*, II, 32.

5. *Chron. Angl.*, 320, 322; *Hist. Anglic.*, II, 31, 34. — *Annales de Dunstaplia*, p. 418. — Stow, *Annales*, p. 293a, 294a.

6. *Chron. Angl.*, 320; *Hist. Anglic.*, II, 31; *Gesta*, III, 347. [Some letters of Richard II dated 17 August (*Claus. 5 Ric. II, m. 39d*) show how much alarm was caused by the apparatus of justice deployed at St. Albans: many of the abbot's tenants who lived in Watford and Rickmansworth had fled for fear of being denounced even though they were innocent. At the request of the abbot, made anxious by this exodus which was ruinous for him, the king ordered the sheriff of Hertford to round up these frightened people and make them return.]

7. *Hist. Anglic.*, II, 36-37; *Gesta*, III, 350-351.

8. *Chron. Angl.*, p. 322-324; *Hist. Anglic.*, II, 35-36; *Gesta*, III, 348-349. — Cf. Pauli, *Geschichte von England*, IV, 533-534.

9. *Chron. Angl.*, p. 324; *Hist. Anglic.*, II, 36; *Gesta*, III, 350. — *Annales de Dunstaplia*, p. 419. — Cf. *Polychronicon*, IX, 7. — *Claus. 5 Ric. II, Pat. 5 Ric. II*, passim.

10. This can be judged from the following description: "Quorum jam corpora, tabe fluentia, scatentia vermibus, putrida et foetentia, odorem ipsis teterrimum refundebant". (*Chron. Angl.*, p. 326).

11. *Chron. Angl.*, p. 325-326 (with the copy of the order of Richard II, which is in *Claus. 5 Ric. II, m. 41*); *Hist. Anglic.*, II, 39-40; *Gesta*, III, 354-355. — [Letters Patent of 10 October 1381, order the release in consideration of a fine of 18 shillings of a certain Thomas, imprisoned at Newgate for having cut down the hanging corpses at St. Albans: Pat. 6 Ric. II, part. 1, m. 21.]

12. Note with what triumph the chronicler of St. Albans reports this deed: *Chron. Angl.*, p. 326; *Hist. Anglic.*, II, 40-41; *Gesta*, III, 355-356.

13. *Patent 6 Ric. II, part. 1, m. 21.*

CHAPTER 7. THE AMNESTY

At the request of Parliament, the king granted an amnesty by a general act dated 13 December 1381, and notified all sheriffs of his decision.[1] Then he published a list of rebels to whom this remission should not apply. For the County of Hertford it was very short, and comprised only four names: William Bilche of Aldbury, John Coltman of Clavering, Stephen Treubody of Codicote, William de Stable of St. Albans. But there were sixteen for Norfolk and eighteen for Suffolk . . .

Reference, Chapter 7
1. Rymer, IV, 136. — Cf. Knighton, II, 151.

THE ST ALBANS CHARTER OF 16 JUNE 1381

Steve Blinkhorn and Gabriel Newfield

INTRODUCTION

This charter was granted at the height of the rising of 1381. It appears in Thomas Walsingham's Gesta Abbatum Monasterii Sancti Albani. As edited by Henry Thomas Riley it is in volume 3, pages 318 to 320 (Rolls Series No 28, Longman, 1869). In the text it is described as a 'Charter of freedom of the villeins of St Alban's forcibly obtained from the Abbot and Convent' (see Note 1). As far as is known it has not hitherto been published in English translation. The present translation is the work of S F B; we have collaborated on the Notes. All place names are rendered as in Riley's text, apart from St Alban's, where the modern name is used, and as indicated in Notes 21 and 37. In the Notes we have as far as possible given their present-day versions and their locations, where these are known. Where locations are not known, but the internal logic of the charter indicates clearly the general area, we have tried to suggest possibilities, having regard to the fact that all the places mentioned must have been well-known at the time and within a limited range of the town. All our guesses and assumptions are clearly shown as such, and should be read as hypotheses inviting confirmation or refutation, and not as probably true statements of fact. We are very conscious of the extent to which we have relied on conjecture to fill gaps in our knowledge. In part this is a comment on the present state of research on Hertfordshire place names, where a great deal of work remains to be done. We would welcome comments on the translation and notes, including suggested corrections or amendments and any evidence which would help to settle the doubtful locations. Such comments may be sent to either of us at The Hatfield Polytechnic. We wish to record our indebtedness to Dr Eileen Roberts, whose work on the topography of mediaeval St Albans has saved us from some mistakes, but those that remain are of course entirely our own.

TRANSLATION

To all children of Holy Mother Church who shall read or hear these presents,[2] we, Thomas, by the Grace of God Abbot of the Monastery of St Alban, and the Convent[3] thereof,[4] wish everlasting salvation in the Lord. Be it known[5] that we, on behalf of ourselves and our successors, have by unanimous agreement and common will granted, and by this present charter confirmed, to our beloved (children) in Christ the burghers of the town of St Alban's jointly and severally, present and future, that they and their successors should have and enjoy in perpetuity each and every one of the undermentioned rights and freedoms.[6] Namely, they and their successors shall have and hold in perpetuity a common of pasture[7] from the town of St Alban's on the high road as far as Stone Crouche,[8] and thence on the high road to Nodaissh,[9] and also from the said town of St Alban's as far as Mileayssh,[10] which is situated on the high road to Luton; also in Barnetwode,[11] in Frytwode[12] and in Dernwellane,[13] on the whole of the path going via Oysturhille[14] as far as Kyngesbury;[15] and from Kyngesbury going via Gounelstone[16] into the said town of St Alban's.[17]

Further we ordain and grant to the said burghers, on behalf of ourselves and our successors, a common of pasture on the high road to Hertford[18] as far as the end of Gonne

Wodelane,[19] and on a certain road a little this side of Gonne Wodelane called "Bemondlane"[20] as far as Rubia Crux,[21] and from there on the whole of the road going via Newlane[22] to St Alban's; and leaving the same town by Tounemandich[23] on the whole of the path to Cranestyl,[24] and thence the whole way to Gryndeslane,[25] and then by the high road to Sopwellemulle,[26] and, next to Sopwellemulle, in the three meadows[27] lying between Flotegatestrem[28] and Mullestrem;[29] and thence on a certain road called "Grenelane"[30] which leads to Fotesplace.[31]

Further, on behalf of ourselves and our successors, we grant to the said burghers two bridleways[32] through Eywode[33] wood, viz one going via Eywodelane,[34] through Eywode as far as Parkstrate,[35] and the other from Parkstrate going through the tenements of John Eywode and Roger Hwcie to Stanesfeldmulle;[36] and one high road from Rubea Crux[37] through Fauntonwode[38] as far as the barn of the Celle.[39]

Further we grant, on behalf of ourselves and our successors, that they and their successors shall be able freely and without hindrance to hunt with dogs and hawks[40] in any place whatsoever within the aforesaid limits and boundaries, whether enclosed or not; and that they and their successors should have a common of piscary[41] from the old fulling-mill which once stood below Eywode as far as the other fulling-mill below the Abbey,[42] and from a certain place called "Sisseborne"[43] as far as the Prae monastery.[44]

And we ordain and grant, on behalf of ourselves and our successors, that they and their successors may keep hand mills either in their houses or elsewhere, wherever seems most convenient to them, and this without denial or trickery[45] on the part of ourselves or our successors.

Further we ordain and grant that our bailiff[46] will not enter[47] the town of St Alban's without the written authority of our Lord the King. In witness whereof we have set both our seal and the common seal of our Chapter to these presents. Dated at the shrine of St Alban,[48] the sixteenth day of June in the fourth year of the reign of King Richard the Second.[49]

Notes

1. 'Convent' in the sense of the monks assembled and meeting in concert.
2. Lit. 'these present letters'
3. The text is ambiguous — the royal *we* may be in use, in which case 'of the convent thereof'. Translator has maintained the ambiguity in his version.
4. Lit. 'of the same place'
5. Lit. 'You shall know'
6. Lit. 'liberties and free customs'
7. That is, common grazing rights on the land in question.
8. Stone Cross, at the junction of Sandridge Road and Sandpit Lane.
9. Could this refer to a Node House, situated at the junction of Sandridge Road, Beech Road and Marshalswick Lane?
10. Could this refer to a Mile House on the 'high road'? The latter is the present-day Townsend Drive and a north-westerly continuation thereof.
11. Bernard's Heath, a wood or heath cleared by burning, i.e. a 'burn'd wode'. Used to be bigger than now.
12. Exact location not known. 'Frith Wood' may mean a coppice wood.
13. Could this be Everlasting Lane? 'Dernwell' means literally a deep or hidden well.
14. Osterhills, just to the north of where the City Hospital now stands. Lit. 'sheepfold hills'.
15. Kingsbury, the Saxon royal fortified dwelling, demolished long before 1381.
16. Gunnerston, originally Gunnar's tun, i.e. Gunnar's enclosure. Various other forms, such as Gomerston

and Gunmerston. The boundary of the town at the bottom of Fishpool Street, near the Black Lion. The recent Gonnerston development is some distance away.

17. Up Fishpool Street, presumably.

18. This seems to be the present-day Sandpit Lane, which is the only old road going in the right direction which is also distinct from Hatfield Road and in the right general position.

19. Running roughly north-south. Could this be present-day Beechwood Avenue or Beaumont Avenue?

20. Assumed to lie, at least in part, on line of present-day Hatfield Road. 'Bemond' is known as a version of Beaumont.

21. Rubiam Crucem in text. Could be 'Bramble Cross' (rubeus = reddish, or made of brambles), or 'Red Cross'. A Red Cross is identified in the usual sources as lying on Sopwell Lane where it meets the town boundary, but 'Rubia Crux' cannot refer to the same place. It must be at the point where Bemondlane becomes or turns into Newlane, on the line of present-day Hatfield Road. Could this be at the junction of Camp Road, Hatfield Road and Stanhope Road? See also Note 37 below.

22. The western section of present-day Hatfield Road.

23. Tonsman Dyke, Townman's Ditch, Townemanditch and various other forms. The earthwork forming much of the ancient boundary of the town, here on the east, following the line of (Upper) Marlborough Road.

24. Exact location not known, but must be in south-east sector. 'Crane' generally refers to the bird, so it is possible that 'Cranestyl' took its name from the presence there of cranes.

25. Exact location not known, but must be in south-east sector. 'Grynd' generally refers to a low place or abyss, so it is possible that 'Gryndeslane' was low-lying.

26. Sopwell Mill, at or near present-day Newbarns Mill.

27. Lit. 'green places'

28. Floodgate Stream.

29. Mill Stream. These references imply a stream used to feed mill races, and a stream with a floodgate, for when the river rose too high for comfort.

30. Green Lane. Not the present one; we have assumed it is the one on the 1634 map, running in a northerly direction towards the town from the site of the now-disused gasworks.

31. This must be in towards the town again, as the final point on this route, but it is not clear where it was. Could it be at or near the junction between Cottonmill Lane and the old road to London?

32. Lit. 'paths for people on foot or on horseback'

33. Eywood or Aye Woods. Lit. 'well-watered and wooded land'

34. Lane leading to Eywood. It is possible that the present-day Eywood Road follows the line of its western part.

35. Park Street.

36. Stankfield Mill, which we take to be at or very close to present-day Cottonmill. A stank is a pool or pond, later a dam.

37. Rubea Cruce in text. The question arises as to whether this is the same point as Rubia Crux (see Note 21 above). If so, then the road in question must have followed by and large the line of present-day Camp Road, and possibly part or all of Cell Barnes Lane. This has implications for the location of Faunton Wood. If, on the other hand, this Rubea Crux is the point where Sopwell Lane meets the town boundary, it would seem that no such road existed at the time — or was ever cut.

38. Faunton Wood, and various later versions, including conjoint name Fawn Wood and Monk Wood. In the general area of Cunningham Hill and The Camp.

39. Cell Barnes, originally a barn or granary belonging to Sopwell Priory.

40. 'Nisus' may more precisely mean a sparrowhawk. Probably used generically here.

41. That is, common fishing rights on the river or waters in question.

42. Presumably at or close to where Abbey Mills now stand.

43. Not identified. The only other known local occurrence of 'Sisse-' is in the manor of Sissevernes at Codicote, whose family were at one time stewards to the Abbey.

44. The monastery out in the meadows. Founded as Hospital of St Mary de Pratis by Abbot Warin of St Albans in about 1190. Later St Mary de Pree, hence Prae monastery. This whole passage must refer to stretches of the river Ver, (a) from somewhere between Park Street and Sopwell to below the Abbey, and (b) from 'Sisseborne' to Prae.

45. Or 'prosecution'. But 'trickery' feels more in tune with the atmosphere of dictating a charter to an unwilling abbot.

46. Lit. 'the bailiff of our liberty', a senior official of the Abbey, second only to the steward.

47. Lit. 'will not insert himself within the boundaries'

48. 'Apud Sanctum Albanum' as distinct from locative case and from 'Villae Sancti Albani'. Implies where the saint is himself, but may be overinterpretation.

49. The text adds "Since the Conquest." Copyright translation © S. F. Blinkhorne. Notes © S. F. Blinkhorne and J. G. H. Newfield.